Regarding Equality

Regarding Equality

Rethinking Contemporary Theories of Citizenship, Freedom, and the Limits of Moral Pluralism

Ellen Freeberg

LEXINGTON BOOKS
Lanham • Boulder • New York • Oxford

LEXINGTON BOOKS

Published in the United States of America
by Lexington Books
4720 Boston Way, Lanham, Maryland 20706

12 Hid's Copse Road
Cumnor Hill, Oxford OX2 9JJ, England

British Library Cataloguing in Publication Information Available

Library of Congress Cataloging-in-Publication Data

Freeberg, Ellen M.
  Regarding equality : rethinking contemporary theories of citizenship, freedom, and the
  limits of moral pluralism / Ellen Freeberg.
    p. cm.
  Includes bibliographical references and index.
  ISBN 0-7391-0154-4 (cloth : alk. paper) — ISBN 0-7391-0155-2 (paper : alk. paper)
    1. Equality. 2. Citizenship. 3. Liberty. 4. Pluralism (Social sciences) I. Title.

  JC575 . F68 2001
  323'.01—dc21

                                                                      2001044097

Printed in the United States of America

♾™ The paper used in this publication meets the minimum requirements of American
National Standard for Information Sciences—Permanence of Paper for Printed Library
Materials, ANSI/NISO Z39.48–1992.

For my husband.

Contents

Acknowledgments

My thanks to Johns Hopkins University and the graduate program in Political Science which supported the initial stages of this work. Bill Connolly and Richard Flathman encouraged an engaging environment for political theorists during my term of study at Hopkins, and for this I remain grateful. To Richard Flathman I owe a particular debt for attentiveness to my work over many years and for ongoing advice, kindness, and guidance.

Thanks also to John Wallach, who has been a supportive friend and colleague; to Pat Neal, who offered initial comments on an earlier draft; and most especially to Phil Green, who has proved to be an extraordinarily astute critic. Phil read the entire manuscript with tremendous care and offered his comments when they were most needed. Needless to say, lingering shortfalls remain my own.

My appreciation to family who have often kept my spirits steady and to special friends Marcy Schwartz, Rick Shain, and Sarah Strong. Jon Powell, my husband, often championed my hardest choices, and his love and commitment have made this project possible. My baby Emma, born shortly after this manuscript's completion, fills my life with the greatest joys and her arrival has made all future projects imaginable.

Introduction

Rethinking Equality

Equality stirs political passions. We use the word to demand elimination of unfair hierarchies, especially based on blood, land, race, wealth, or gender. We champion it in order to challenge institutions to govern through fewer arbitrary conventions, to make comparisons based on relevant criteria pertinent to a job or practice. Equality represents a familiar hope. It promises fairness. It seems an unlikely source for complaints, an unquestioned promoter of cherished goals.

Yet equality's virtues face formidable critics, especially of late. Some writers produce elaborate arguments urging us to avoid the term based on its conceptual conundrums. Others cite the concept's dangers (Pennock and Chapman 1967; Westen 1982, 1990). Ironically enough, while equality talk has faced some sustained skepticism from conservative-oriented thinkers (Bell 1972), many recent critics identify with left-leaning political tendencies and sustain deep commitments to social justice. The latter generally have supported equality as a higher-order goal, yet now often talk of rejecting it to expand opportunities for diverse and excluded voices in democracies like our own.

Feminist legal theorists have stood at the forefront of such critiques, especially through their analysis of court cases about pregnancy in the workplace (Bock and James 1992, ch. 1; Mansbridge and Okin 1994, part 2). They have tried to show how appeals to equality can hinder real opportunities for fairness, blinding us to relevant differences or excluding legitimate talk about distinct needs.[1] The problems go beyond gender as well. Others believe neither distinctive physical challenges nor cultural considerations have been well served by abstract characterizations of "sameness." Equality may prod organizations to

1

root out arbitrary biases in hiring by remaining blind to differences (wheelchair use, for example). But the "blind to differences" goal may ironically undermine what looks like fair, even if different, treatment. Classic equality approaches, so the complaint goes, demand too much assimilation and too little recognition and accommodation of distinctive needs.[2]

Where does this leave egalitarians? Should they reassess their commitments altogether? Or should they use these observations to remind us that equality, like so many political ideals, is an ambiguous achievement?

An answer is not simple. And it appears more complex after confronting work by theorists like Carol Pateman (1988) or Iris Marion Young (1990). Not only do these thinkers reinforce the practical dilemmas noted above. They also demonstrate links between current concerns and the liberal tradition. From the seventeenth century through the enlightenment and through early work by John Rawls, the moral and political assumptions of the liberal social contract tradition have justified public policies based on choices imagined by equals characterized as free based on their ability to abstract from class, race, culture, and gender. Rawls's *A Theory of Justice* (1971) had, of course, emphasized the importance of this forgetting, while reinforcing how a process of abstraction through an original position was neither degrading nor diminishing of distinctiveness. We all share the capacity to form particular (yet rational) purposive life plans. Simultaneously we can assess the universal rightness of these plans. We accomplish this by "veiling" our prejudices and finding the most neutral vantage point possible from which to settle on fair rules for all. Any attempt to destabilize or dismiss such a process only leaves us subject to the clash of self-interest and the resolution of conflict through sheer might rather than legitimate, self-governing consensus.

For Young and Pateman, Rawls and others like him sound well intentioned. But liberals like Rawls expect all to function with impartial and universal moral reason. This exemplifies the dangers of traditional liberal equality. As Young puts it, this approach will "reduce the plurality of moral subjects and situations to a unity by demanding that moral judgment be detached, dispassionate, and universal." As she explains further, "reducing differences to unity means bringing them under a universal category, which requires expelling those aspects of the different things that do not fit into the category. Difference thus becomes a hierarchical opposition between what lies inside and what lies outside the category, valuing more what lies inside than what lies outside" (1990, 102). Traditional strategies actually pursue unfair expectations because they construct sameness in ways that exclude alternative conceptions of moral reflection—and then they fail to explore how their exclusions have occurred and what unfair consequences may result. Such critiques do not necessarily mean complete rejection of "the universality of moral commitment, expressed in the assumption that all persons are of equal moral worth," as Young puts it. But "universality in the sense of the participation and inclusion of everyone in moral and social life does not imply universality in the sense of the adoption of the general point of view that leaves behind particular affiliations, feelings, commitments, and desires" (105). Equality talk may appeal, but it needs rethinking.[3]

If credible, such critiques put egalitarians on the defensive. Nevertheless, while taking current anxieties seriously, this essay insists that several contemporary tendencies in political thought—identified here as strong, liberal, and deliberative democratic—offer characterizations of equality that look highly attentive to reducing assimilation and promoting generous accommodation of moral pluralism. Represented by work from Amartya Sen and Martha Nussbaum, John Rawls's writings post-1985, and Amy Gutmann and Dennis Thompson, the positions reviewed here do not simply align themselves with one monolithic trend toward simple assimilation. As Amartya Sen has put it, few serious political theories can avoid the question "why equality?" or ignore efforts to justify why and how we should be treated similarly. Indeed, even those who so carefully deconstruct equality often return to forge their own abstract characterization of sameness. (Young (1990, 37) does this all too briefly.) Hence, this essay sets out to clarify and contrast several contemporary theorists who tackle the "why equality" question[4] and who do so with particular care as well as with responsiveness to new demands for fairness.

A second and more distinctive goal sets out to outline specific difficulties with the three approaches noted and to broaden current debate. Strong, liberal, and democratic positions try to expand fairness via inclusion of different moral perspectives. However, each position faces a series of internal dilemmas that diminish pluralism-sensitive ambitions. These dilemmas revolve around a particularly pressing issue: namely, how to characterize our shared capacities for freedom.[5] The foundation for strong, liberal, and deliberative democratic equality relies heavily on claims about our shared capacity for autonomy. And autonomy proves a demanding, moralized view of positive freedom. In contrast, I argue for also valuing agency-centered descriptions of freedom. I have no doubt that agency-centered orientations, conceived less in terms of virtuousness and more in terms of modest expectations about a "situated," purposive conception of the self (Flathman 1987), have appeal, especially when moral diversity and the conflicts it produces within democratic societies are both strong and valued. However, I urge caution when supporting more complacent renditions of agency as represented by a thinker like Michael Oakeshott. I draw from Oakeshott in an effort to characterize agency as it relates to our broader capacities to imagine, shape, and pursue distinctive goals. I also see the attraction of Oakeshott's expectations for what I will call an ethic of equality leading to "civil regard" toward others. The ethic helps mitigate as it maintains strong moral pluralism. But I would add to this. Even a modest conception of agency can and should champion not just civil regard but what I call "responsive regard" for others. The latter should commit us to fostering understanding and civility toward others; and to protecting against obstacles that hinder external action and potentially degrade our capacities to imagine and maintain self-esteem. Purposive individuals deserve protection against various types of harms in order to have an equal chance to act on their desired goals. Moral philosopher Susan Brison and legal theorist Drucilla Cornell help reinforce these points as well. Unfortunately, Oakeshott tends to ignore or at least not address their concerns directly given his limited views of power and his excessively limited view of how much we can know about one another given the formal rules and practices we share.

Autonomy-centered thinkers, as I am calling them, do understand their potential pitfalls. They recognize how a "positive" freedom tradition invites charges of 1) excessive fear regarding the human capacity to act upon rapacious self-interested desires; 2) a tendency toward paternalism, especially for those identifying freedom with the close pursuit of collective moral ends; and 3) a certain limited critical analysis of public institutions and their role in promoting collective virtues. However, chapters 1 through 3 demonstrate how strong, liberal, and democratic egalitarians, while sensitive to these classic dilemmas, often fail to overcome them satisfactorily.

Sen and Nussbaum, for example, maintain a highly substantive conception of what we share. We share a capacity for autonomy. But autonomy refers less to (negative) "agency freedoms" and more to (positive) "well-being freedoms." Our well-being is met (and hence "real" freedom achieved) when we are able to meet certain functions (to escape premature morbidity, to have adequate nourishment, to have proper shelter, etc.). Such functionings derive from the (often biologically) necessary needs and goals that humans share across cultures.

Unfortunately, such views stand especially vulnerable to dilemmas 2) and 3) above. Sen and Nussbaum hope to sidestep problems with classic (neo-Hegelian) positive freedom positions by ignoring efforts to label as unfree those who are characterologically impoverished or fall short of virtuous conduct based on shared traditions. Sen and Nussbaum, nonetheless, cultivate a highly perfectionist stance and retain the necessity of "enabling" those who fail to reach or place a premium on the goals associated with well-being freedom. In addition, while this approach offers implicit support for a highly developed welfare state, which we may applaud in certain circumstances, such a direction needs on-going critical scrutiny. Recognizing such concerns, Nussbaum argues that no one should fear excessive state interference or reasonable limits on cultural diversity with the "capability ethic." Developing a list of universal functionings can look almost morally agnostic or metaphysically uncontroversial. Chapter 1 concludes, otherwise, however. Even though Sen writes that "the assessment of the claims of equality has to come to terms with the existence of pervasive human diversity" (1992, 1), the capability ethic generates significant tensions between its universal claims and the cultural particularities it hopes to override.

Rawls's political liberalism may seem more promising in contrast. Early on, Rawls supported a classic, Kantian view of personhood and autonomy. Kant, of course, never expected rational beings to demonstrate freedom through attunement to communal norms or biologically necessary ends. Kant saw acting rationally and freely bound up with acting rightly. And he understood righteousness not in relation to the pursuit of common substantive ends but in relation to our capacity to transcend particular perspectives through the application of a formal rule identified as the categorical imperative. Rawls later distanced his ideas from this "comprehensive" and universal conception of autonomy. To sustain the strongest possible (yet still reasonable) level of moral diversity, a liberal political theory was said to need virtuous, autonomous citizens only in specific, limited instances—when constitutional issues were at stake. Rawls's "political liberalism" could say this and then claim to avoid replacing one strong perfectionist oriented position (Hegelian in character) with another (indebted to Aristotle) (Nussbaum 1990a).

However, as chapter 2 argues, a closer review of the criteria through which political liberalism supports even a limited conception of equality as autonomy leads to disappointments. Rawls may have rightly acknowledged the need for greater receptivity to the diverse beliefs voiced in liberal democracies. But he fails to convince readers that a previously Kantian conception of autonomy can meet certain internal standards (remain limited, freestanding, and culturally circumscribed and therefore nonmetaphysical) in order to attend to strong levels of moral pluralism.

Gutmann and Thompson acknowledge such problems—and aim to reformulate Rawls's ideas. They reinforce how individuals share an ability to pursue their own ends; but simultaneously emphasize how individuals qua self-legislating beings must participate in the *actual* decision-making processes that shape the rules governing their lives. As free, individuals require political participatory virtues such as the capacities for public speaking and effective conversation with others. Furthermore, good public speaking requires the exercise of "reciprocity" marked by "civic integrity" as well as "magnanimity" and "openness" toward others with whom we disagree. Such deliberative virtues are neither neutral nor limited in scope. But they respect diversity particularly well, the claim goes, because they remain sensible and keep face-to-face conversation *going* before decisions solidify. Such expectations will not try to *translate* differences into a scale of functioning capabilities; nor will they ask us to *transcend* differences in order to legitimate public principles before conversations begin. Reciprocity hopes for greater understanding between us after civil conversations ensue. Perhaps conversation will *transform* differences and provide new mutual understandings. But reciprocity remains formal—it tells us how to speak, but not exactly what to say. It should never interfere, therefore, with anything but the most unreasonable of speakers and life plans.

Chapter 3 applauds these efforts. It supports talk of equality in relation to freedom as conditioned by practices and enhanced by participation in the rules shaping conduct. It also supports the link between freedom and intelligent speaking, freedom and conduct based on awareness of the civil expectations of certain practices. But it remains concerned about these demands, notably with reciprocity's vision of openness and its goals of achieving deep mutual understanding through deliberation. Deliberative democrats implicitly demand a high level of what I call transformative openness from individuals participating in public dialogue, and while not always undesirable, this may not fully appreciate the "disharmony" of democracy, as Gutmann calls it. As chapter 4 suggests, deliberative democrats fail to explore thoroughly enough how the moral pluralism they value must account for disharmony marked by moral incommensurability. When moral incommensurability is strong, serious breakdowns in understanding exist. Following suggestions from Joseph Raz, Bernard Williams, and others, chapter 4 argues that incommensurability can exist in degrees, may limit significantly assumptions used to bridge differences between distinct "social forms," and should require varied tactics for the mitigating conflicts that result. In some cases, requests to resolve differences by exercising political autonomy with its attendant virtues will look viable, perhaps even desirable. In other circumstances, more chastened expectations such as simple acknowledgment of another's capacity for agency marked by intelligent action and agreements to remain civil (or just let others be) may look more attractive.

Chapter 5 explores these further suggestions. It points toward characterizations of freedom in terms of agency in contrast to autonomy. It discusses the way situated agents can bridge differences through an attitude of civil regard as discussed by a thinker like Oakeshott. An agency-centered/regard-oriented ethic deserves attention, I claim. But while Oakeshott helps in this effort, his ideas may not prove most attractive since they rarely account for the substantive conditions needed to attain even a modest view of agency. Chapter 6 expands on this problem, arguing that a description of agency (even if identified with a less demanding notion of reason and virtue) should still draw attention to our common needs to imagine and pursue our goals; subsequently, it should provide ways to identify and limit significant obstacles that hinder our use and exercise of such capacities. I reinforce this point by discussing links between agency freedom and the avoidance of degradation of physical integrity as well as preservation of something like what Drucilla Cornell calls an "imaginary domain." Agency remains an achievement. As a result, chapter 6 expands on the harms we should protect against if agency is valued. It also develops the case for an ethic of civil regard with "responsiveness" toward others. The latter focuses on encouraging civility and an enlarged appreciation for others. It acknowledges the need for access to rules and resources that an agent, situated in a particular practice, may require in order to flourish. In the end, I will not suggest that my ideas promote a fixed list of necessary conditions for agency development. I will, however, claim that valuing agency can promote more than Oakeshott imagines; and "responsive regard" for others should prevent a range of obstacles to project pursuits while it enlarges access to concrete resources that actors need in order to use the rules integral to a shared practice. Distributive justice and issues of material well-being need not be ignored when moral pluralism becomes a preoccupation (Fraser 1997, ch. 1).

Overall, this essay provides a comparative review of well-known positions in contemporary political philosophy that defend cherished, often liberating efforts to recognize what we share and accord individuals dignity. Such efforts stand out as a well-known, inspiring part of modern political philosophy. Past efforts have not always served satisfactorily. But this need not prompt rushed dismissal of all characterizations of equality. I contrast familiar as well as new possibilities here. Other options exist and hopefully the discussion as framed still welcomes additional, contentious interventions.[6]

Notes

1. Of course, feminism has struggled since its inception over such issues related to equality. See Nancy Cott 1987.

2. This distinction between assimilation and accommodation will come up again. Generally put, I associate assimilating with the incorporation or conversion of something into another, of changing one thing such that it can be absorbed into and become identical with another. Accommodating suggests making room for something or someone, giving consideration to the other and perhaps reaching a settlement in the midst of differences.

3. Stanley Fish, 1999, would disagree. Highly sympathetic to Young's type of critique and her political inclinations, Fish nonetheless would say Young and those with similar concerns should totally reject equality talk as capable of promoting universal principles of inclusion and fairness for democratic institutions. Fish proves a harsh critic of equality and his pragmatic alternative is discussed very briefly in chapter 4.

4. There are clearly other components to an equality analysis that could be reviewed (Williams 1962). Sen deals briefly with the justification for equality and wants to talk more about the "equality of what" issue, meaning he is concerned about the variables we should use when trying to measure equality. Do we establish this measurement based on gains and losses of utility, libertarian negative rights, or a liberal distribution of primary goods (Sen 1992; also see Alexander and Schwarzchild 1997; Arneson 1989; Cohen 1989; Daniels 1990)?

5. Thinkers like Peter Westen will claim that this derivative relationship of equality in terms of freedom makes equality talk superfluous. It is true that one can convincingly discuss equality relationships only with reference to a third variable or standard (or a rule). Persons A and B are always equal with respect to some things. Hence, adding equality talk to any analyses may not only be derivative but create confusion or "distortion." "After such a rule (or third variable or standard) is established," Westen writes, "equality between them [persons] is a logical consequence of the established rule. . . . [Persons] are also . . . entitled to equal treatment under the rule because that is what possessing rule means" (Westen 1982, 548).

Equality conceptually does remain derivative, but does this render it superfluous? Responding to thinkers like Westen, Jeremy Waldren has written of equality's force in historical and not only linguistic contexts (Waldren 1991, 1363, 1365). He has directly questioned critics who fail to say enough about equality's rhetorical use and who cannot abide by any ambiguity in political language (1366-67). Moreover, he is not fully convinced that "some deep idea, conventionally labeled 'equality' or 'equal concern' might not form the basis of many important arguments in politics favoring the choice of some distributive principles over others" (1367). Here Waldren cites Ronald Dworkin's reliance on the notion of equal concern and respect, and he notes that while thinkers like Westen refer to Dworkin, and others like Bernard Williams, attention to these thinkers and their commitments to equality are not addressed as fully as one might like. "Certainly," as Waldren argues, "we could formulate our convictions using different words. We could say that respect is due humanity as such. But equality has the extra and important resonance of indicating the sort of heritage we are struggling against. We believe in a profound respect due to humanity, and we maintain that belief in the face of those who claim that humanity admits of degrees" (1363). Amartya Sen has made complementary points. Modern moral or political theories owe something to a notion of equal concern and respect for persons; this is always posited as the fundamental variable for interpersonal comparisons, as part of an "abstract egalitarian plateau" (to use Dworkin's phrase). Moreover, every contemporary theory, committed to some ideal social arrangements, has to be "credible from the viewpoint of others—potentially all others" (Sen 1992, 17) and talk of equality reinforces this. To do away with equality because of its formal or messy qualities sounds foolish to Sen. Other concepts like justice may have a formal character, but we do not dispense with them. Instead we clarify what they depend upon. If derivative, they are not necessarily debased.

6. I recognize the limits of the discussion as constructed here. But I think the contrasts and possibilities provide important starting points for reflection. Other interesting options could come from a thinker like Jane Flax. In her 1995 "Race/Gender and the Ethics of Difference, A Reply to Okin's *Gender Inequality and Cultural Differences*," Flax talks about resisting the Rawlsian approach to equality and respect for difference contrasting this with an ethic that encourages us to see ourselves as others do, unsettle any feeling of being "at home" with our perspectives, and to "decenter" the self in order to promote respectful engagements with different others. Flax only gestures toward these possibilities, but they set up provocative beginnings.

Chapter 1

Strong Equality

Amartya Sen and Martha Nussbaum characterize equality based on the assumption that all humans share a capacity for freedom, specifically what Sen calls "well-being freedom." For them, too many moral and political theorists assume we share "agency freedom" ("the realization of goals and values [a person] has reasons to pursue, whether or not they are connected with her own well-being" (Sen 1992, 56)). This is not enough. As a starting point, it remains too stingy and cautious. It leads primarily to limited rights and negative protections. Real equality and standards of decency and fairness *depend upon* first achieving a highly substantive threshold of well-being. This threshold should be discernible across historical and cultural divides. All humans need to achieve "valuable functionings" (such as being well nourished, sheltered, or clothed) and, when *made* capable of these (as well as other) basic functionings, humans are then really free, able to pursue their diverse (individual) goals effectively. All societies should understand this and use their public institutions and resources to promote achievement of such substantive ends.[1]

It stands to follow that a person malnourished often lacks the ability to care about voting (or to get to a voting booth). This chapter remains highly sympathetic to such points. But the "capability ethic," as Sen (1992) and Nussbaum (1990a) call it, faces significant attacks from negative freedom supporters, dubious about how well we can sustain individuality alongside a "positive" conception of freedom demanding that some "enable" others. It also faces charges of insensitivity to diversity from anti-essentialists or postmodernists concerned about biased, often western-based, metaphysical assumptions underlying a list of human functionings. And traditionalists question whether enabling can occur

9

without attention to more particular local customs and interpretations. I do not claim to embrace any one of these critical perspectives in toto. I do, however, think each presents significant concerns. In the end, the capability ethic claims its use of an a priori list of shared human functions accommodates widely different interpretations of how to achieve well-being. But I claim that supporters of the ethic face troublesome trade-offs and limitations.

This chapter divides generally into two parts. I initially focus on the critical questions posed by negative freedom supporters and how Sen especially responds to them. I enlist Richard Flathman's work (1987) to criticize positive freedom and suggest ways in which the capability approach must (and does not) address Flathman's analyses. The second part of the chapter turns to questions about metaphysical foundations and responsiveness to local traditions. Nussbaum tries to show how the capability ethic tackles these concerns (esp. 1992). In the end, her points are less convincing than one would hope. I agree that we may share some capacities for freedom and that meaningful equality requires access to the substantive conditions for free action established within different practices. But the capability ethic with its requirement to enable achievement of abstractly formulated conditions (necessary for all times and places) remains more difficult to justify than proponents suggest.

Agency and Freedom

Positive vs. Negative Freedom

Sen and Nussbaum believe that all humans qua equals share the desire to be free—but what does this mean? And how to achieve it? Freedom relates to our ability to pursue distinct life plans. But this, in turn, depends upon achieving a set of common goods, needs, or values first. We must be given the opportunity or, as Sen and Nussbaum see it, we must be enabled to be well nourished, properly sheltered, protected against preventable diseases, capable of pleasure and pain, enabled to meaningfully participate in our communities (Nussbaum 1990a, 1992). Freedom requires a vision of what we should do or be (a version of "positive" freedom).

As such, the capability ethic faces critics who see it as conceptually incoherent and morally undesirable. Those critics say that equality based upon freedom as the pursuit of individual ends cannot be so tightly linked to achieving such a robust list of collective values or needs. To enable the latter sets too many limits on the former. Moreover, we may wish to support collective institutions that limit external impediments and support civil liberties. But these institutions become much more contentious when invested with authority to enable and establish a threshold for "normal" capabilities. In the end, views of positive freedom promote too many interventions and remain too dangerous for a society that treasures diversity and individual expression.

Positive freedom proponents would see themselves mischaracterized here. Sen responds more fully. He recognizes concerns that positive freedom is theoretically and semantically "a confusion, since freedom is quintessentially concerned with the absence of restraint and interference by others" (Sen 1988, 273). But he believes this is

> a somewhat odd claim, since the positive characterization of freedom is not only coherent, it also corresponds closely to a person being actually free to choose. It is not, contrary to some claims, a "modern" distortion of the idea of freedom, and it can be seen not only in many 18th and 19th-century writings, but also in many earlier contributions, e.g., in Aristotle's analysis of the role of freedom of choice in *Politics* and in *Nicomachean Ethics* (1988, 273).

More specifically, the semantic arguments fly in the face of common sense:

> It is possible that the difference (between positive and negative freedom) may partly be one of terminology only. Even if, for some reason, the term freedom were not to be applied to the positive characterization of what people tend in fact to do or be, it is possible nevertheless to argue that those positive features may well be of importance. For example, when discussing the case of an "ordinary citizen. . . not being able to buy an object which he does not have money enough to pay for", Frank Knight remarks that it is "a clear misuse of words" to describe this "as a deprivation of freedom". He prefers to describe it as a "deprivation of power". Yet elsewhere—not inconsistently with his view regarding the definition of freedom—Knight chastises utilitarians for overlooking "the fact that freedom to perform an act is meaningless unless the subject is in possession of the requisite means of action, and that the practical question is one of power rather than a formal freedom". It can, thus, be argued that substantively it may not matter precisely how freedom is defined, so long as the importance that the positive characterization freedom deserves to have is attached to whatever alternative term—in this case "power"—is used to refer to the same thing (273).

Elaborating in "Well-being, Agency, and Freedom," Sen adds that positive freedom "effectively boosts our power—while negative freedom affects individual control. The latter, again, proves insufficient. It often "does not matter for freedom as control whether the person succeeds at all in achieving what he would choose" (Sen 1985, 209). On the other hand, freedom

> assessed in terms of the power to achieve chosen results (is concerned with) whether the person is free to achieve one outcome or another; whether his or her choices will be respected and the corresponding things will happen. This element of freedom, which I shall call effective power. . . is not really concerned with the mechanism and procedures of control. It does not matter for ef-

fective power precisely how the choices are "executed," indeed choices may not even be directly addressed. Effective power can take note of counter factual choice: things might be done because of knowledge of what the person would choose if he actually had control over the outcome (208-9).

Sen continues: "It is often not possible to organize society in such a way that people can directly exercise the levers that control all the important aspects of their personal lives. To try to see freedom exclusively in terms of control is to miss out on the demands of freedom when control cannot feasibly be exercised by the persons themselves" (210). He also expects positive freedom to incorporate negative concerns:

> In matters of what to eat, what to drink, what to wear, it may not be adequate just to get what one would have chosen; one must actually do the choosing oneself. However, it is, in fact, also possible to argue that if achievements are characterized in a more articulate and apposite way than they are in the conventional formulations, then the motivation underlying any intrinsic concern with the control element of freedom can be subsumed within the notion of the power to achieve results (212).

So individual rights and protections should be available but with other conditions in place that actually enable *meaningful use* of negative protections.

If you believe our greatest needs have to do with controlling our choices and avoiding certain kinds of impediments, you have produced modest expectations about freedom, and too few options for improving equality to its fullest. Again Sen: "if a person happens to be poor and hungry because of low real wages or unemployment, without his having been prevented . . . from seeking a higher wage or finding employment, then the person's negative freedom may not have been, in any way, violated, even though his positive freedom from hunger is clearly compromised by circumstances" (Sen 1988, 272). Negative freedom supporters may talk of respect for others as abstract, self-interested persons, and may support certain rights and liberties, but they provide little hope for promoting substantive duties. Adherence to a negative conception of freedom is theoretically "thin," politically vapid, at best, politically incomplete.

Kinds of Freedom and Free Agency

Richard Flathman's *The Philosophy and Politics of Freedom* offers a detailed analysis of what is often meant by positive and negative freedom. Flathman remains highly skeptical about positive freedom but presents his objections from an especially sophisticated starting point. After outlining several of Flathman's challenges (he believes the positive freedom tradition presents an incoherent view of human desires, a misguided view of rule following, and a troublesome link between a strong capacity for rationality and freedom), we can explore how the capability ethic responds. If the latter tackles some of Flathman's challenges reasonably well, it would seem poised to thwart initial skeptics.

Flathman assumes, first, the need for revision of any simple positive/negative freedom dichotomies. In their place, imagine a continuum. This goes far toward better critical analysis and understanding. Identify freedom1 (F1), as a classic or "pure" negative position represented by Hobbes, Flathman suggests. The latter talks of freedom as "self-activated movement plus the possibility of impediments to the movement in question" (Flathman 1987, 322 for a list of kinds of freedom). Freedom2 (F2) stands as a modified negative form. It envisions free (and unfree) actions (and impediments) as possible only if taken by agents (the latter envisioned as individuals who have intentions and desires modified by rules and norms and able to reason and exercise understanding to at least a minimal extent). Freedom3 (F3) represents a weak positive freedom. It may add to the agency requirement of F2 the necessary capacity to pursue "a self-critically chosen plan or project," not just any intention, desire, or interest. As free agents, we should also believe that our projects are "consonant with defensible norms or principles." Freedom4 and freedom5 would add the weighty demand that plans or projects in freedom3 "be chosen to satisfy, and in fact (are) satisfying, norms or principles that are authoritative in the agent's community" (F4) or "certifiably worthy" (F5). (Hegel through Charles Taylor represent this end of the spectrum.) F4 and F5 would stand as robust positive freedoms in Flathman's continuum.

These observations do more than clarify. They reveal stark negative and positive poles as conceptually misguided or unintelligible, often politically unappealing. Ironically the purest negative and positive freedoms share assumptions about desires that give behaviorism too much clout. F1 insists that freedom exists only when movement propelled by inner states is externally unimpeded. On this view, the self's inner desires, passions, or interests are discussed as mental or physical states, but never as complex expectations, forms of reflection, deliberation, or interests in a particular object (46-47). F1 also obviously fails to see anything within the self moderated by rules, norms, or shared principles. This presents an incoherent view of the self as actor. Furthermore, F1 not only starts with incoherent assumptions about human desires, but it cannot distinguish between movement that just "happens" to a self with or without consent and movement impelled intentionally or with reason. You catch your heel in the pavement and fall. Is this a "free" act? I stop you because I happen to be in front of you. Have I made you unfree? Supporters of F1 say yes. Flathman (and he assumes an ordinary language user) says no.[2] F1 fails to support agency as we can and should understand it. F1 fails to describe movement that looks "freedom evaluable" (ch. 5).

F4 and F5 do no better. And here lies the first major problem with positive freedom. Opposing F1, positive freedom proponents often take the latter's assumptions about desires for granted. F4 and F5 usually (tacitly or otherwise) talk of desires as brute urges. They contend that such urges compel or "enslave." Freedom becomes possible only if the self can rationally order and control its base inclinations or heteronomous demands. But desires only "enslave" if viewed reductively. The behaviorist trap snares positive freedom supporters too, from Kant and Hegel through Gerald Dworkin and Charles Taylor. Freedoms4-5 go on to demand that the self, who properly orders inner forces, desires, etc., attune him or herself to the rationality and morality of collective norms or rules. Flathman admits that desires, indeed all actions, remain situated by rules and norms. But freedoms 4-5 give an implausible account of situated action. They "underestimate the extent to which the most precisely formulated norm or rule . . . leaves scope for variation in conduct." "Even rules that form a 'strict calculus' (Wittgenstein) take the agent by the elbow, not by the throat," as Flathman reminds (23). Taylor's distinctive perfectionism leans toward fusing freedom with the need to incorporate highest-order, worthy social goals and virtues (deeply and definitively) into one's character. Such requirements misunderstand rules and make unreasonable demands on us, or at least promote cruelties and opportunities for blame that should be acknowledged, if not abandoned. More strongly put, to make attunement to communal norms a requirement of freedom misunderstands what it means to be a free agent living in a society that values pluralism. Positive freedom is a "moralized" view of freedom, descriptively misguided, and with respect to rule-following, obnoxious and politically dangerous.

With these critiques noted, one might instead endorse F2 or F3. F3 defines freedom in relation to autonomy, a trait admired in our society and perhaps the basis for valuing freedom (see, for example, Raz 1986). But there are obstacles to consider with this as well. Humans do demonstrate a capacity for rationality and self-assessment. And many political theories, rightfully influential in our society, prize on-going reflection about political (and other kinds of) authority. Yet should autonomy and strong rationality be valued but not necessary requirements for agency and participation within a diverse polity?

At least two significant points could limit linking autonomy with effective agency. First, while autonomy and rationality (the former always presupposing a high level of the latter) can be worthy achievements, it is not clear that we require rationality in a strong sense in order to qualify as an agent. On most construals, autonomous action involves a very strong capacity for reason. "In particular, autonomy involves making and acting on rational assessments of more than one's own ends and choices of means and more than the actions of others with whom one is directly involved" (Flathman 1987, 206). But as Flathman tries to point out, numerous habitual, potentially "irrational" behaviors can prove unfortunate, perhaps self-destructive, often unfathomable, but should not be disqualifying of agency. Flathman outlines a host of "irrational" behaviors that we would likely agree still involve degrees of choice and action (ch. 4). He dwells at one point on the example of the religious individual who may fail to exercise strong rationality and/or critical reflection, but who could not plausibly be labeled unfree or in need of internal correction (though this could be the un-fortunate message of F3). Flathman also offers an extended argument against thinkers such as Bernard Gert who tend to reinforce the need for autonomy by insisting on a universal standard of rationality in order to assess freedom or un-freedom. While "it is true," Flathman notes, "that the rest of us often must assess A's performances, including her claims and laments about coercions" and "it is also true that we cannot do so without employing some standard of judgment" (213), general standards for reasoning need not be presented as universal nor should they "require rationality of the agents and actions they are used to as-sess," Flathman argues.[3] Intentional action should be associated with agency; rationality only more or less.

This first problem with autonomy relates to its weighty notion of rationality. A second suggests that freedom and autonomy can prove incompatible, even deeply conflictual. Two corollary points highlight this. i) While cultivation of autonomy may seem consistent with freedom, efforts to make individuals more self-conscious or critically reflective often do lead to compulsory programs and interferences. It is not completely obvious that all such programs are to be ap-plauded or seen as wholly consonant with freedom (see Flathman's examples 219-20). ii) Autonomy is usually considered an "ideal of character" (297). It may not be easily distributed or protected with assurance. We should exercise caution in protecting it alongside civil liberties and rights. This is not to say that freedoms could never aim to protect autonomy. Or that at times we may be, as Flathman notes, "justified in promoting autonomy at the expense of freedoms of action" (298). But a person could enjoy numerous rights and privileges as the equal of others in his or her society, yet never attain autonomy. Moreover, Flathman also points to the way freedoms of action concern most humans as purposive actors while autonomy does not (297). And he cites the way some who rightly wish to promote a "self-reflective and self-justifying political soci-ety" (particularly thinkers such as James Fishkin) incline too quickly to establish conditions for an autonomous citizenry, conditions that then remain insulated from debate (301-2). This last move troubles since it suggests that positions placing extraordinary value on self-rule and self-justification can often under-mine the very things they prize.[4]

These are key stumbling blocks for positive positions with perfectionist claims. Add to this Flathman's effort to establish a more sophisticated negative freedom position, one committed to seeing individuals as agents "situated" or governed by what Joseph Raz calls "social forms" or what Wittgenstein labels "forms of life," and then the claim that position freedom is incoherent sits along-side a fairly sophisticated alternative defense of negative freedom. (Flathman, part III)

But some might say that thinkers like Flathman make neo-Hegelians the tar-get of their critiques. Those who borrow from Kant or J. S. Mill—or Aristotle—remain less interested in having individuals become free through attunement to collective virtues. Can an Aristotelian-influenced capability ethic alter the positive freedom continuum and avoid the problems raised?

Equality of Functioning Capabilities

The capability ethic incorporates three notable tactics to avoid the strongest versions of positive freedom and their problems.

First, neither Sen nor Nussbaum suggest that desires simply enslave. Desires may be manipulated, but this occurs often in relation to external conditions imposed by oppressive political regimes. Unlike classic positive freedom proponents, Sen and Nussbaum place less direct emphasis on the inner world of the self as chaotic, controlled by brute desires in need of excessive inner control or rational ordering.

Second, Sen and Nussbaum avoid emphasizing attunement to particular, local communal virtues. They commit to formulating shared ends, but these are seen as historically widespread or "natural" to all as biological organisms with certain shared capacities. If anything, Sen and Nussbaum often resist elements of the communitarian tradition inclined to lament modernity and our inability to rediscover or reconnect to the shared understandings of a tradition.[5]

Third, as far as the relationship between positive and negative freedom goes, both try to balance the two. While concerned about what people can actually do, Sen writes in earlier articles that "(i)t can . . . be argued that the deliberate violation of one person's freedom by another is something that is especially obnoxious and the special disvalue may call for particular attention being paid to violations of negative freedom even when the overall positive freedoms are much the same" (1988, 275-76; 1999 18-19). Sen's latest book goes further and frequently claims to value liberal rights—or the "intrinsic" importance of political freedoms associated with liberal democracies (1999, ch. 6). It overtly resists arguments from political elites, especially in East Asian societies, who have claimed that implementation of political liberty and civil rights (or even "human" rights) remain unnecessary given their country's particular need for economic growth as well as their drive to preserve traditional, "nonwestern" values. (1999, ch. 6 and 7).[6]

All of this appears to circumvent familiar problems. However, dilemmas lurk. Start with one, primarily descriptive, identified with both positive and (pure) negative freedom proponents: the willingness to slip into talk of unintentional movement as free or unfree. While Sen and Nussbaum seem to avoid talk about desires as brute or identify "movement" (versus action with intention) as free or unfree, Sen does write the following rhetorical questions in an effort to critique negative freedom:

> Why should our concern stop only at protecting negative freedoms rather than be involved with what people can actually do? Should one be under an obligation to save the person who has been pushed into the river but not the person who has fallen into it? . . . In deciding whether one is under an obligation to

help a starving person, should one say "yes" if the person has been robbed (with his negative freedom being violated) but remain free to say "no" if he has been fired from his job, or has lost his land to the moneylender, or has suffered from flooding or drought (without any violation of negative freedom) (1984, 314-15)?

Sen wants to establish an obligation to help both the person pushed and the one who has fallen, the person whose food is stolen and the person starving as a result of drought. But are these obligations exactly the same in both cases? Are both individuals to be helped because both have been made unfree?

Natural disasters create undeniable powerlessness and misery. These are conditions due a response. But the question is whether these always can be understood as conditions of unfreedom (and properly used to calculate our standing as free agents). Moreover, it may not be possible to readily equate the slip or fall with all the other nuanced conditions (losing a job) that Sen discusses. Aren't there degrees of unfreedom here shading into problems of powerlessness?

Sen admits at one point that some of his ideas may create confusions. But, as was seen earlier, Sen is quick to add that "it can . . . be argued that substantively it may not matter precisely how freedom is defined" (1988, 273). What should concern us, he suggests, is whether the "positive characterization of what people can in fact do or be" is given importance, at least taken into account in policy making. So, whether we call this condition freedom may not make a difference. But then why bother conflating unfreedom with powerlessness or something else? Why the unnecessary confusion?

The answer is presumably bound up with a desire by both Sen and Nussbaum to place the capacity to achieve basic needs and physical functionings on the same level as civil liberties (Sen 1999, 64). Or, again, as Nussbaum puts it, the tension between care for well-being and the value of choice is "to a great extent, illusory" (Nussbaum 1990a, 238). Many such basic needs do deserve our attention (collectively) and much more so than some classic liberals admit. But to get at this concern by equating fulfillment of a somewhat controversial universal set of needs with real freedom may not prove so easy. Given points made earlier, it is unlikely that in the example above my involuntary slip and fall into the river is simply about a situation that shows my inability to act as a free agent. To ignore this seems to strain common sense while effacing a workable notion of agency (and possibly a more contextually specific, acceptable understanding of what constitutes the social goods we are likely to want to distribute in an effort to sustain equality) (see Walzer 1983).

These points hint at conceptual confusions that draw the capability ethic closer to F4 or F5. But if this does not do immediate damage, it does intensify questions. In Sen's example above, we find that the person who is pushed should be helped or aided differently from the one who just falls. And this is because the act of enabling or helping the person pushed is unlikely to request an agent's permission before helping or enabling. It seems right for you to dive into the water and pull me out—without asking my permission—if you see me trip involuntarily, fall in the water, flail about and start to scream. In fact, there is little else you (or another) can do in order to help. If, however, we are concerned about the pushing that occurs on the water's edge, we can establish certain rules, perhaps rights, in advance that deter actions and give some individuals ways to help themselves before they fall in. Of course, this does not change the moral obligation some would identify to help the person pushed in. It highlights, however, that one kind of situation likely involves individuals more so in their capacity as actors. The other situation sees them severely diminished and subject to more paternalistic assistance. Doesn't making capable (and deciding in advance what constitutes functioning capabilities) involve serious limitations on choice that may prove controversial and/or undesirable? And what if I resist being made capable and taken care of in the way you think best for me? What provisions are made for such resistance? Little, it seems, if the goals are "elementary" (Sen 1999, 75) and necessary for all. And even if I did agree to being made capable, who makes me capable? Is there no concern here with the ambiguity of authority?

Nussbaum repeatedly uses certain examples to respond. Fasting may be a reasonable choice; it means you choose not to eat but can still attain food. Starving is different; food sources are unavailable, or you cannot use them properly. Moreover, clean water and safe food must be available and you must be capable of using such resources adequately. We would unequivocally want governing authorities to ensure as much. So concerns about authority evaporate when making us capable of necessary functionings because the latter are *so essential* and because no one will make you achieve the functionings if you do not wish it (Nussbaum 1999, 44).

But this makes the problem too simple. The language of enabling implies a level of involvement in someone's life that may be reasonable in desperate situations but not in others.

In the case of starvation, concern about enabling pushes us to think beyond simply sending money or food supplies. It asks us to consider who controls roads for transporting food, whether some needing nutrition are pregnant, whether others are so incapacitated that they will need nutrients intravenously. And if starving you might not worry about someone else pumping food into you the best way they know how and having others make assessments about the threshold for normal nutritional intake for your particular body type. But assume that lack of steady work produces a scarcity of food in a family—not necessarily starvation but significant strain and hunger some days. This situation may be addressed, first, by giving public funds for food. The capability ethic would likely see this as insufficient and want to enable us to get out of poverty and achieve adequate nutrition. Maybe enabling here makes us think more comprehensively about building major transportation avenues from isolated neighborhoods to corporate centers. This could occur alongside cash for food programs like food stamps. But there is always the potential, if *making able* is the ethic (and not just providing opportunities given a particular practice or activity) that the individual who does not take up the opportunities offered has to be evaluated, questioned, convinced, perhaps helped along if inadequately utilizing resources leading to a worthy end. What if some use public food stamps to buy cigarettes? Smoking diminishes nutrient absorption. If being adequately nourished is an obviously valued functioning, we might prohibit using food stamps for tobacco or alcohol purchase. Or to enable fully we might go further and require counseling for smokers or drinkers so they can see their nutritional intake as dangerous, a shameful degradation of their bodies. Again, a certain degree of correction can be implied by enabling. And then important questions do crop up: what level of authority or government should be involved in these processes of enabling; is instruction or correction of a certain kind occurring mainly for those most vulnerable or receiving state subsidies; what about the problems of cultivating a client-based relationship between state bureaucracies and individuals rather than one more expressly engaging individuals as citizens and democratic participants?

The capability ethic could escape some such issues if able to convince us that a circumscribed list used to define our needs is "essential" enough and that we would almost never deny letting others promote its components. Is there a list of functioning capabilities objective in some such sense while flexible enough to use in particular instances and respond to a variety of cultural contexts?

Nussbaum's work tries to address this more fully. Sharing much with Sen it offers a slightly more direct answer to the justification issue and defends a universal consensus on a list of functioning capabilities.[7] Sen hints at support for such a list but remains ambiguous about its contours and its "metaphysical" status (1985, 197-98). Nussbaum commits to an extensive philosophical defense of "constitutive circumstances of the human being" (mortality, living with a human body, having the capacity for pleasure and pain, needing humor, play, separateness as well as affiliation with other humans, etc.) (1990a.) and how these generate all the necessary functionings that humans should be able to reach. While linking such ideas to Aristotle, Nussbaum tackles concerns about harboring a controversial metaphysic (1990a, 206, 217-18; 1992, 206-8, 214-15), and she answers charges that her list cannot be highly pluralism sensitive or thoroughly capable of accommodating different groups within a society like her own or elsewhere.

Enabling Essential Human Functionings

Dismissing Metaphysics, Avoiding Controversy

Throughout her work, Nussbaum presents a set of "constitutive circumstances" or "grounding experiences" common to all humans. These are readily discovered (1988a., 40) and likely include our shared human confrontation with: mortality, the general limits faced by the human body, the need for experiencing pleasure and avoiding pain, the need for early infant development and eventually certain human social interactions, and the need for recreation, laughter, and play, to name a few (1990a., 224-26). These help us establish necessary human functionings and then these imply which necessary capabilities we should have in order to perform these functionings well. If we all face the experience of mortality, we should all consider it essential "to be able to live to the end of a complete human life, as far as is possible; (to avoid) dying prematurely, or before one's life is so reduced as to be not worth living." Given the shared vulnerabilities of the body, we should all wish "to have good health; to be adequately nourished, to have adequate shelter." And so on (1992, 222), each general observation leading to a specifically formulated goal.

As for defending the noncontroversial status of such ends, Nussbaum claims that 1) an "internal essentialist" foundation for such a list can avoid controversial metaphysical or religious understanding of the self and human history; and that 2) the list can incorporate commitments to cultural diversity and personal choice, something demonstrated when looking at the capability ethic put into practice.

Of course the first question is whether this "thick" theory of "the good" can really rest on a noncontroversial metaphysic. In particular, if Nussbaum turns to Aristotle for support, does her position rely upon understandings about the human animal or human virtues difficult to promote across many moral and cultural boundaries (whether within a society or across nation states)?

Nussbaum could reject Aristotle's biological assumptions for a multicultural democracy, say. But she could insist on selective use of such ideas. Anticipating problems, however, Nussbaum makes a more complex defense. She insists on a distinction between a controversial metaphysic ("metaphysical realism") and an "essentialism" that remains noncontroversial (1992, esp. 206-8). Nussbaum says the capability ethic is essentialist since it claims objectivity as well as universality. But it proves reasonable by basing itself on a comprehensive analysis of human lives and histories, and not, like metaphysical realism, by discovering a fixed order detached from human experience. The question should not be, how does the capability ethic mask attachment to a (possibly Aristotelian) metaphysic, but what specific "humanist" assumptions inform the foundation of "internal essentialism," as Nussbaum has called it? And what do we make of their status?

The controversial versus noncontroversial distinction of metaphysical realism versus essentialism needs clarification. Presumably metaphysical realism also uses religious or specific moral assumptions for grounding a general definition of well-being. Justification for these assumptions will be based on a limited consensus, one that fails to sift through and appeal to the rich details of human history, the only "facts" we "know." A noncontroversial (nonmetaphysical yet essentialist) foundation, on the other hand, should discuss individuals qua historically situated humans. Generally accepted facts about human nature (not necessarily tied to Aristotle) should be relied upon (215). Nussbaum discusses two such social facts as critical: first, that "we do recognize others as human across many divisions of time and place"; and second that "we do have a broadly shared consensus about the features whose absence means the end of a human form of life." On the latter, Nussbaum continues: "We have in medicine and mythology alike an idea that some transitions or changes just are not compatible with the continued existence of that being as a member of the human kind (and thus as the same individual, since species identity seems to be necessary for personal identity)" (215). While not value neutral, these points about recognition and consensus can ground well-accepted understandings about all humans.

This should appeal to common sense. In addition, it leads to a list of capabilities that "allows in its very design for the possibility of multiple specifications of each of the components." In other words from these we identify a notion of well-being with room for "plural specification" and "local specification" (224). Finally, those who would claim otherwise have little else to offer. They either rely on similar assumptions but fail to acknowledge as much. Or they "collapse into" a morally degenerate and untenable subjectivism, offering no ideas of their own about our common needs (209-13; also 1999 ch. 1). Does this approach rest on fewer than expected assumptions indebted to Aristotle? Does it convincingly justify its facts about the human condition?

The Problem of History Reconsidered

It remains difficult to dispute the "fact" that we can (and must) recognize other humans across "language games" found within one culture and even across time and space. We often find examples of mutual recognition in our widespread outrage against senseless killings, torture, or other forms of brutality. But do these moments of common ground rest on assumptions that can lead to what Nussbaum calls "cross-cultural attunement" (216) about essential human abilities? And can a universal set of shared understandings provide for ways to overcome but not eliminate diverse viewpoints, at the very least within societies like our own?

Nussbaum would say that we can and must express more than solidarity with others. We go beyond this in large part because of the second "fact" cited earlier: that "we have a broadly shared consensus about the features whose absence means the end of a human form of life." How to gain a consensus about such features? Often Nussbaum suggests little difficulty in gathering information and finding consensus. From "the stories told by Greeks about the Olympian gods" (216) to the plays written by Shakespeare, we can recognize universal themes about the human condition discussed across time and space. "Especially valuable are myths and stories that situate the human being in some way in the universe . . . stories that ask what it is to live as a being with certain abilities that set it apart from the rest of the living beings in the world of nature, and with, on the other hand, certain limits that derive from our membership in the world of nature" (215). Nussbaum continues: "The great convergence across cultures in such recognitions and refusals of recognition gives us some reason for optimism that if we proceed in this way, using our imaginations, we will have in the end a theory that is not the mere projection of our own customs but is also fully international and a basis for cross-cultural attunement" (216).

But if this method for collecting data leads to more than limited recognition of common fears, and if it is supposed to produce positive not just negative duties, and if it leads to such a detailed list of necessary functionings and abilities, we do need a fuller explanation about how to discover such convergence. We need a better description of Nussbaum's favored historical or anthropological method for analysis.

Nussbaum talks occasionally about how to decide "whether (a) function is so important that a creature who lacked it would not be judged to be properly human at all" (1988b, 177). At one point she notes, "(t)he question is answered like any other Aristotelian ethical question: namely, by looking at the evaluative beliefs of the many and the wise" (177). This is evasive (and given Nussbaum's attempt to dissociate herself from Aristotle's metaphysical biology and his ethical views of women and slaves, the passage may be even more difficult to decipher). However, Nussbaum does try to say more through examples. She talks of a linguistic analysis supporting her position in the following way:

> We begin with some experiences—not necessarily our own, but those of members of our linguistic community, broadly construed. On the basis of these experiences, a word enters the language of the group, indicating (referring to) whatever it is that is the content of those experiences. Aristotle gives the example of thunder. People hear a noise in the clouds, and they then refer to it, using the word "thunder." At this point, it may be that nobody has any concrete account of the noise or any idea about what it really is. But the experience fixes a subject for further inquiry. From now on, we can refer to thunder, ask "What is thunder?" and advance and assess competing theories. The thin or, we might say, 'nominal definition' of thunder is "That noise in the clouds, whatever it is." The competing explanatory theories are rival candidates for correct full or thick definition. . . . There is just one debate here, with a single subject (1988a, 37; also see 1988b, 178).

Once we identify key terms—like the recurring words for "mortality" or "death" found in other known languages—as well as the experiences that prompt them, shared human concerns emerge. But the question still is not only whether this linguistic analysis can work, but, if it is plausible, whether one can narrow the range of shared words and experiences in order to get a clear and universal list?

Nussbaum goes further to clarify in "Aristotelian Social Democracy," discussing an "A level" list of "constitutive circumstances of the human being" (1990a, 219) and then a second "B level" list from which the "basic human functional capabilities is derived" (1992, 222). Justification of the A level list introduces two main dilemmas for Nussbaum's noncontroversial foundation: 1. reliance on a highly circumscribed set of historical sources; and 2. gestures toward a certain kind of "internalist" historical method.

The first concern emerges from the footnotes justifying each grounding experience on the A level list. The list of experiences includes, but is not limited to, some of the experiences mentioned earlier: mortality, capacity for pleasure and pain, cognitive capacity, certain early infant development needs, the need for humor and play. Of the fifteen footnotes that support reasons for citing these and other key experiences, all refer to observations from ancient Greek writers (1990a, see notes from 52-67). So, for example, when Nussbaum writes that "(t)he experience of the body is culturally shaped; but the body itself, not culturally variant in its requirements, sets limits on what can be experienced, ensuring a lot of overlap," (220) the reference cited for support is Aristotle's view of the unity of soul and body. The pattern continues as Nussbaum talks of more specific limitations on the body (hunger, need for shelter, sexual desire, etc.).

I would not say Aristotle's observations lack any appeal to contemporary common sense. And Nussbaum's scholarship in ancient thought is unquestionably impressive. But a high standard has been established by talk of essentialism. A reference to Melanie Klein on early child development amidst the numerous references to Aristotle, Plato, or Epicureanism may offer too little to suggest that the rich details of various human histories are taken into account (1990a, n. 59). Given an inordinate privileging of observations by ancient Greeks, Nussbaum may sound unreasonable when claiming that "refus[al] to assent" to her position will likely come from those "who have not been willing to engage in the cross-cultural study and the probing evaluation that is behind the list" (1992, 223). According to her own demands, Nussbaum may have sidestepped these probing evaluations required for universality. It is also not enough to say now that a list of functionings is rooted in a broad "consensus" because it "resembles" lists derived in (two) other countries also committed to a humane welfare policy (1992, 223; 1990a, 240).

Nussbaum might counter by acknowledging the limits of her discipline. She is not an historian and can only gesture toward the kind of history that supports her position. She mentions Charles Taylor several times throughout various discussions, and in a review article (1990b, 34), she references Taylor's sweeping "internal" history of western moralists with its commitment to finding common "sources of the self." Reservations about Taylor's work surface, but Nussbaum finds much in it to commend.

Taylor resists "reductive strategies" in social thought, notably associated with behaviorism and utilitarianism. They ignore the importance of complex goods that give life meaning. Modern moral identity, and indeed politics, "tends to sink" into the despair of fragmentation if our most important understandings are left unacknowledged or "unarticulated." Higher goods as we know them emerge from "frameworks" (Taylor 1989), distinctive ways of life or "defining communit(ies)" (Nussbaum 1990b, 36). "Western civilization" has produced numerous such frameworks: theological, utilitarian, Marxist, to name a few (Taylor 1989, 23). But the differences between them should not mask the shared set of "higher order goods" (respect, dignity, and the need for a worthy life with a particular orientation to the good) critical to any. There are goods "which are most widely adhered to in our civilization, have arisen through a historical supersession of earlier, less adequate views—analogous to the critical supersession of premodern by modern science"; and such goods "are understood by those who espouse them as a step to a higher moral consciousness" (Taylor 1989, 64). As "hypergoods," these have had a varied, complex articulation throughout our history. It is the job of the moral philosopher to locate and articulate them.

This "internal" search for hypergoods through our western history Nussbaum cites with praise. Taylor's history has its own ontological debts, notably to Hegel (1975; 1989). Taylor's more recent discussions in *Sources* regarding "historical supersession" of a particular view of rationality (1989, 68-74), and even attunement to a vaguely described form of spirituality (1989, ch. 4 and 25), should sound unsurprising then. Nussbaum holds out Taylor as a "close relative" on these points (1992, n. 12; n. 36). She embraces his anti-relativism. Her key quibbles relate to his limited use of "sources." Western ideas need not provide the sole source for our highest values, she claims. "Only a more extended account. . . will tell us how to assess tensions in our current set of ends, how to decide which are fruitful, which are the result of arbitrary and dispensable elements," Nussbaum writes. "And this becomes more urgent still if we wish to take in the entire human world. Taylor's account applies only to views that succeed one another within a continuous history" (1990b, 34).

So, the capability ethic must improve upon Taylor's "internalist" essentialism. But again, has this occurred? Don't such protests ring slightly hollow in light of Nussbaum's own limited historical inquiry? Even if we overlook this, how could Nussbaum account for the moral sources Taylor privileges ("to deny them this role is to impoverish our own possibilities") (1990b, 32) and support Taylor's views about narrative and identity, while also claiming common ground between these ideas and the "oral traditions, myths, stories and self-understandings" of other (often less powerful) voices? Nussbaum's main critique of a thinker like Taylor is that he does not include enough marginalized voices in his development of hypergoods, a point well taken. But can all voices become part of a grand narrative, a global story which leads to a distinctive set of shared ends without relying on some progressive understanding of history? What if valued ends in one culture do not show any overlap with what we believe are "more truly neutral" (1988a, 38) articulations of the things we identify as shared ends or experiences? Either Nussbaum expects all of human history to converge on the "more truly neutral" shared values and cannot explain how that will happen—except through some form of historical progress. Or she masks the way her own historical justifications for essentialism depend on highly circumscribed sources.

Flexibility in Practice?

Nussbaum insists that amidst the multiplicity of human cultures, "plural specifications" and diverse interpretations exist over how to pursue various functionings (see 1988a, 37; also see examples in 1992, 234). "Plural specification means what its name implies. The political plan (based on the capability list), while using a determinate conception of the good at a high level of generality, leaves a great deal of latitude for citizens to specify each of the components more concretely and with much variety, in accordance with local traditions or individual tastes" (1992, 224).

Take for example "the fear of death, the love of play, relationships of friendship and affiliation with others, even the experience of the bodily appetites." Nussbaum writes that "these never turn up in a vague and general form, but always in some specific and historically rich cultural realization, which can profoundly shape not only the conceptions used by the parties in these areas, but also their experience itself, and the choices they will make" (1990a, 234-35). "Corresponding to each of the vague functionings there is an indefinite plurality of concrete specifications that may be imagined, in accordance with circumstances and tastes" (235).

This does not reject scrutiny of cultural norms. Indeed, a community may introduce tactics (vaccinations, for example) in the name of promoting capabilities, and adversely affect traditional norms or ways of thinking (belief that a certain god could cure the ailments now prevented by the vaccine). Some critics have charged Nussbaum's move in this direction stifles cultural autonomy. But Nussbaum counters:

> The Aristotelian, while not wishing to interfere with the capability of citizens to use their imaginations and their sense of the purposes of religious expression should they choose to do so, would certainly make bodily health a top priority and would not be deterred in a program of smallpox vaccination by the likelihood that it would eradicate the cult of Sittala Devi. The Aristotelian would introduce the vaccination scheme and then leave it to the citizens to see whether they wished to continue their relationship with that goddess (1992, 234).

Introducing a vaccine, in this example, accords with expanding choice. Cultural norms may be altered due to certain health policies. But in so doing, individuals choose to alter these norms, and in most cases cultural integrity need not be destroyed, Nussbaum says (1992, 208-9; also see 1999).

What about choice at the individual level? Again, critics have charged that "by determining in advance what elements of human life have most importance, the essentialist is failing to respect the right of people to choose a plan of life according to their own lights, determining what is most central and what is not." Among her responses, Nussbaum insists repeatedly that: 1. individual "practical reason" remains a top priority on a list of basic functionings and 2. freedom must continue to be defined not simply in terms of a spontaneous ability to choose, but in terms of the conditions that enable individuals to choose.

Practical reason does show up on Nussbaum's list of human functionings. In Nussbaum's words, it is "architectonic" (sharing this position with only one other functioning, our need to affiliate with others). It "both infuses all the other functions and plans for their realization in a good and complete life" (1990a, 226-27). To enable any of the necessary functionings, then, requires attention to an individual's capacities to evaluate and plan for him or herself. Governments may use the capability ethic to maintain a clean water supply. But individuals could pollute the water they pour into their own cup. Likewise, "[a] person with plenty of food can always choose to fast; a person who has access to subsidized university education can always decide to do something else instead" (1992, 225; 1999 esp. 43-47).

In "Aristotelian Social Democracy" Nussbaum also discusses four specific policy areas related to labor, property, political participation and education, and in each case, tries to show how policies can enable freedom (as the ability to exercise individual choice) alongside well-being. On education policy, for example, governments can bring individuals up to a level of basic functioning while avoiding paternalism because:

> Education is required for each of the major functionings; and it is required, as well, for choice itself, as the Aristotelian insists. One distinctive sign of the Aristotelian conception, with its intense focus not only on functioning but also on truly human functioning within the various spheres of life, will be its tendency to make education a, perhaps the, central focus of planning, and to judge success in this aspect to be the hallmark of a successful political design.
>
> The Aristotelian approach will be to specify vaguely certain capabilities that we wish to develop in citizens through education, and then, as Aristotle puts it, to behave like good doctors, looking responsively at the needs and circumstances of the varied groups of citizens and designing the structures of education in such a way as to bring them to those capabilities (1990a, 233-34).

However, we find coupled with the discussions on labor, property, and political participation continual use of references to Aristotle to develop specifics. The examples could but do not move from a) developing a general list with its emphasis on things like the need to be "able to imagine, to think and reason," to b) exploring specifics about our own or any other specific contemporary society in order to deduce what would be required to promote various functionings. Rather Nussbaum assumes that something like education to enable thinking and reasoning will be promoted and in a way discussed by Aristotle. The discussion of education continues with comments such as the following: "He (Aristotle) envisages a combination of a more or less uniform public structure with a more flexible private education provided in and by the family" (1990a, 234). When more details are offered about property "rights" the following is suggested:

> In addressing himself to this question Aristotle never seriously considers the possibility that all ownership should be private. This he considers highly divisive, inimical to sociability, and subversive of the stability and security of the polity. He considers, as we have seen, various combinations of common and private ownership, schemes where some private ownership is combined with common use, and also (as the agrarian nature of his polity requires) schemes in which some of the commonly owned land is held by individuals who are in charge of developing it. What he asks in assessing these various forms is, what makes human functioning best? Or to take his other way of putting the question, what is it to treat citizens as free and equal (234)?

These points do not simply endorse Aristotle's general form of reasoning. They promote the content of Aristotle's ideas. We might agree with Aristotle's suggestions. But why rely so heavily on them? Are they appropriate to all cultures? Nussbaum has not suggested otherwise.[8] If we are to leave room for "plural specification" in practice, at least in this one important section on specific policies, the capability ethic does not indicate a clear commitment to cultural pluralism. Again, it does not even draw from ideas associated with Nussbaum's own culture in order to show how the "vague" but necessary capabilities lead to specifics.

Cultural autonomy seems less clearly demonstrated here too. The emphasis on practical reason also may not satisfy the concerns voiced earlier that individual autonomy looks less secure. Recall that practical reason refers to our ability to plan and evaluate and it should assume significant weight in relation to other functionings. This presupposes a certain view of agency. But how does Nussbaum imagine agents expressing their wants, needs, or goals? She rejects a desire-based approach. Desires are highly corruptible, too often manipulated and subject to exploitation (see examples 1992, 229-30). To trust an individual's evaluation of his or her needs or wants is not impossible; clearly, an individual as an agent must be properly informed or situated before his or her desires prove reliable. However, when or in what kinds of situations do desires seem reliable? Unfortunately, Nussbaum talks in vague terms about when and how to assess trustworthy desires. "The good lawgiver's list of functionings will not be altogether independent of human desires and preferences," she writes at one point, "for the various excellences are defined in terms of the preferences of a certain

sort of human being, the person of practical wisdom." The person of practical
wisdom is somehow more "reflective" than others. "The reflective evaluations
this person performs are likely to differ considerably from the unreflective or
defectively reflective, preferences of most people," Nussbaum writes (1988b,
154). But what does it mean to be defectively reflective? A strictly Aristotelian
understanding of the term could be unacceptable given Aristotle's exclusive
view of who can and cannot reflect wisely.

This limited description of human agency poses problems when we go back,
as well, to Nussbaum's definition of freedom. Recall that an ethic of making
others capable emphasizes the importance of conditions for being able to make a
good choice. As a result, public authority when used to improve capabilities
should not appear as oppressive as many suggest. But degrees exist to which
government involvement in individuals' lives remains compatible with freedom.
At times, Nussbaum acknowledges this (1992, 221, 225). Other times, not. With
a vague commitment to distinguishing between reliable and unreliable individual forms of self-expression, it is troubling to find such an easy connection made
between actions taken by government authority and the promotion of freedom.

Nussbaum might remind us that she has listed other basic functionings—
strong separateness, for example—to help ensure a sphere of individual privacy.

> Separateness and strong separateness have been read here to require the protec-
> tion, around each citizen, of a sphere of privacy and non-interference within
> which what goes on will not be the business of political planning at all, though
> politics will protect its boundaries. What is in this sphere and how far it extends
> are matters for political argument; but the Athenian interpretation of this idea
> was that it included almost all speech, above all political speech, most of family
> and sexual life, and most, though not all, of one's dealings with personal
> friends (1990a, 239).

Nussbaum expects to go further, noting that an "Aristotelian conception" in
order to remain consistent with its "intuitions about strong separateness and
choice" should move "in the direction of a scheme of basic rights of the person"
(239). But does the language of rights remain compatible with a position deeply
indebted to Aristotle? When Nussbaum has discussed private property, often
understood in terms of rights in our society, she has stated the following: "If
someone can show the Aristotelian that the particular kind of context of non-
interference that separate functioning really requires does not, in fact, include
private ownership, then the defense of private property, thus far, collapses"
(232). Presumably, if the goal of a right can be reached in ways other than respecting its exercise, Nussbaum does not expect to maintain the right. But this
does not seem totally in keeping with the way many think about rights these
days (Flathman 1980).

Sen and Nussbaum assume that as needy, interdependent creatures, humans particular interests exist alongside a set of more general goals that all would wish to achieve in order to be well off and equally capable of free choice. However, sanguine expectations about shared goals or capacities, often highlighted in positive theories of freedom including Sen and Nussbaum's, need to address concerns. Sen responds to conceptual as well as political concerns raised about how well his theory sustains commitments to diverse individual expression. But questions remain about the content and universal justification of any position that sees essential human functionings as naturally necessary to achieve (or be capable of achieving) prior to all individual pursuits. Reviewing Nussbaum's general list of functionings points to ambiguities about its justification as well as its expectations for preserving moral and cultural diversity.

John Rawls and other self-described "political liberals" have, over the past decade, presented challenges to Sen and Nussbaum, but without compromising substantive concerns about equality—or so they claim. Liberals like Rawls have often argued that a pluralism-sensitive egalitarianism can emerge from a characterization of "personhood" based on more limited assumptions than the ones considered in this chapter. Claims about our common needs, ends, or goals are implausible, political liberals argue, if conceived as describing something about our essential nature or our fundamental humanity. We should, instead, imagine ourselves as free and equal, but present any commonalities as practically necessary, not philosophically true; as products of a current consensus developed over time in our particular society, not as universal; as limited to discussions about what we need as citizens, not associated with what we need as humans or even as members of every private moral or religious group to which we belong.

In the chapter to follow, Rawls's formidable version of free and equal personhood along with its attendant ethic of respect is explored. Reviewed many times over, the position remains significant since Rawls refined his later work to respond to concerns about accommodating moral pluralism. Part of Rawls's refinement involved rethinking the Kantian roots of his theory and without simply turning to a negative freedom position. Does political liberalism provide a method for transcending our differences via another view of freedom that relies on autonomy but insulates itself from problems in the capability ethic?

Notes

1. The questions I raise throughout this book—and the views from other contrasting thinkers reviewed—generally assume a more parochial audience than Sen and Nussbaum do. Implicitly, I am aiming, at the very least, to characterize commonalities for a multicultural society more like our own, not for societies severely famine stricken, for example. Sen and Nussbaum do think globally. And their work should be seen as emerging from a deep commitment to helping countries economically deprived, although they would want to see their ideas appropriate for a fairly cohesive western liberal democracy

like our own, I believe. Sen, for example, targets his ideas toward philosophers in the Western tradition as well as development practitioners worldwide (see especially 1999). More often than not, both fail to properly help people who live in dire situations. The utilitarians, and the economists who draw from this tradition, might be concerned about well-being but only the sum total of happiness rather than how well-being may be unequally distributed; the Rawlsian liberals and their allies fail to see that liberty cannot take priority when people are intensely poor (and even a generous distribution of certain "primary goods" falls short in helping individuals facing vastly different circumstances and with different abilities to convert the resources to their best use). While I will end up wary of how well the capability ethic can balance enabling alongside individual choice (and how this may hinder the position overall), I would acknowledge that Sen and Nussbaum's ideas may prove more appealing if used in situations where severe deprivation persists.

2. Flathman's later writings take a more sympathetic turn toward Hobbes (see Flathman 1993) and in ways that I expect would alter some of his claims in his book on freedom. Such suspected alterations would, from my perspective, remain much less appealing.

3. Flathman continues here: "In general, human beings are coerced if threatened with death, severe pain, bondage, and so forth. It is therefore rational to employ such threats when trying to coerce someone and reasonable to treat such threats as excusing the performance of those subjected to them. But some people are indifferent to or welcome death; pain thresholds and the capacity to tolerate pain vary; prison has been said to be the just person's proper place in an unjust regime; on a cold night jail may be the preferred abode of derelicts."

4. "There is a paradox lurking here that can be put in the form of a question: how can a society committed unqualifiedly to freedom of political discussion (and autonomy) exclude any remotely political beliefs or arrangements from such a discussion, let alone what on Fishkin's account is its most fundamental political arrangement? Fishkin's liberties are among the basic institutions or arrangements of the society; as such his own argument would seem to forbid (on pain of loss of legitimacy) regarding them as beyond criticism" (301).

5. This becomes ever more apparent in Nussbaum's latest work (1999), which makes considerable efforts to criticize religious traditionalists who dismiss talk of human rights, especially for women (see especially ch. 3). In this same book, Nussbaum challenges Will Kymlicka's efforts to preserve cultural minority rights (108-9), and she defends a rigorous critique of cultures engaged in genital "mutilation" (ch. 4). Sen's latest book also defends the capability ethic and its universalistic functioning capabilities against those traditionalists from the "Asian values" debate (see 1999, ch. 10).

6. Sen argues that democratic political freedoms have value in and for themselves, but 1. can potentially assist economic growth (1999, 150), 2. have never been rejected in toto by citizens in third world countries in favor of authoritarian rule, as some would lead us to believe (1999, 151), and 3. may remain familiar even to certain traditional Asian communities if one looks carefully at the history of the region (1999, ch. 10).

7. I realize that these brief comments on Sen do not do justice to his oeuvre. Clearly I use selective elements of Sen's work, those especially important in defending the capability ethic against negative freedom critics. (In general, Sen has done this more fully than Nussbaum.) However, for the most part, I find Nussbaum offers political theorists the

more full-blown philosophical justification for the capability ethic. As a result, it should not surprise readers that her version receives particularly close scrutiny here.

8. Nussbaum does move closer to supporting traditional elements in liberal theory in her latest book on social justice (see 1999, esp. ch. 2). But how this creates tension with what had been and still incorporates a social democratic vision of justice indebted to Aristotle remains a bit elusive.

Chapter 2

Liberal Equality

John Rawls's liberal political theory has consistently struggled to secure commitments to equality alongside appreciation for moral pluralism. Rawls's talk of placing "the right" before "the good" encapsulated this effort. More specifically, for my purposes, Rawls has spent considerable effort over several decades refining his definition of our shared minimum capacities or the "moral personality" traits necessary but "not at all stringent" (Rawls 1971, 506) for identifying who counts as the "sort of beings . . . owed the guarantees of justice." In *A Theory of Justice* Rawls described these assumptions more fully in relation to human capacities for rationality and reasonableness—the former describing our capacity for "a conception of [the] good (as expressed by a rational plan of life)"; and the latter describing "a sense of justice, a normally effective desire to apply and to act upon the principles of justice, at least to a certain minimum decree" (1971, 505). Promoting a "partial" perfectionism, this approach hoped to avoid dilemmas faced by Sen and Nussbaum with their "thicker" conceptions of the good, but it simultaneously expected to promote "the respect which is owed to persons irrespective of their social position" (1971, 511). Rawls added to this an account of "primary goods" needed to exercise moral personality. But these would be limited to general "rights and liberties, powers and opportunities, income and wealth" (62), with the latter given less priority in Rawls's eventual dual-level just principles.

Originally, Rawls claimed tremendous inclusivity for his description.("There is no race or recognized group of human beings that lacks this attribute. Only scattered individuals are without this capacity, or its realization to the minimum degree, and the failure to realize it is the consequence of unjust and impoverished social circumstance, or fortuitous contingencies" (1971, 506).) But he simultaneously used later writings, notably the 1980 Dewey Lectures, to clarify how his assumptions (1971, 251-257) drew from Kant's ethics. This additional point worked, in many ways, to Rawls's disadvantage. His work became all the more open to criticism from liberals concerned about the exclusivity of Kant's virtue ethics. And, of course, he faced efforts in the 1980s to dramatically expose Kantian-influenced ethics as deeply biased, unable to include "different" voices and therefore illegitimate as a characterization of moral personality (Gilligan 1982; Okin 1989a). The lectures of *Political Liberalism* (1996) strove to steer clear of such concerns and to reinterpret Rawls's theory as truly appreciative of the wide ranging "comprehensive moral doctrines" populating liberal democracies. The question here is how well these goals were accomplished.

For my purposes, *Political Liberalism* developed two acknowledgments of significance. First, the book demonstrated Rawls's determination to focus on the "problem" of moral incommensurability or breakdowns in interpersonal comparability. Second, Rawls no longer wanted to risk grounding his ideas on a full-blown metaphysical version of positive freedom, in this case linked to our real "nature" as autonomous beings, possibly dependent upon presuppositions about Kant's noumenal self. The values of our "political culture" should be discernible by the astute moral philosopher and used to form a pragmatic, "political" conception of free personhood. The latter would present a limited "public" construction, distanced in its demands from our diverse "private" moral points of view but able to keep opposing perspectives among us committed to the virtues of toleration and political order. Moral pluralism, then, could be sustained so long as the assumptions leading to a public conception of the person never proved too demanding or unfairly offensive to many different (non-Kantian inclined) others. But how well could political liberalism reach its quest for balance here? How could it preserve some virtuous conception of autonomy alongside recognition of a high degree of moral incommensurability?

As far as this chapter is concerned, an answer requires analysis of the self-imposed demands on political liberalism that ensure its "political yet nonmetaphysical" character. Rawls political conception of the person, and hence the foundation of his theory, claims to be broadly acceptable to citizens and Western democracies so long as it remains: 1. limited in scope or "framed to apply solely to the basic structure of society, its main political, social, and economic institutions as a unified scheme of social cooperation"; 2. freestanding or "presented independently of any wider comprehensive religious or philosophical doctrine"; and 3. guided by practice or "elaborated in terms of fundamental political ideas viewed as implicit in the public political culture of a democratic society" (Rawls 1996, 223).[1] Are these demands sustainable? Not as cleanly, as political liberalism requires.[2] And the ambiguity in Rawls's distinctions diminishes political liberalism significantly. Yet, the generosity of political liberalism's accommodations of pluralism and the distance it places between its notion of autonomy and Kant, depend upon such distinctions being carefully preserved.[3]

Moral Personality and the Promise of Pluralism

What does it mean, then, to envision a notion of free personhood limited in scope? In brief, it means that most of the time—in most "nonpolitical" situations—individuals should be left to determine their goals and choose their own moral perspectives. In other situations, in a range of highly circumscribed, clearly public situations, individuals should adopt a different perspective. They should acknowledge how everyone can and should be capable of exercising two moral powers associated with being autonomous in the liberal sense as Rawls has defined it.

The plausibility of this brief answer depends upon two interrelated claims. First, Rawls believes individuals can and should occupy roles self consciously, well aware of the demands they face in different settings. Second, and more specifically, individuals should discern which roles are political versus nonpolitical, which concern public as opposed to private life, which ask us to envision ourselves and others with the capacity for autonomy as opposed to any other form of freedom (one defined, say, as attuning oneself to godly commandments).

Political liberalism must then make sense of the distinction between political as opposed to nonpolitical understandings. "The political" may very well be a distinct space, appropriately identified with a particular role, set of duties or requests. But controversy always swirls around definitions of the political. In Rawls's case it now becomes much more important to dissociate the political from the nonpolitical or private sphere since in many respects Rawls's characterization of moral personality still looks just as it did in his original theory of justice. What should save Rawls's characterization of free and equal personhood is the idea that it need only apply to narrowly circumscribed behaviors.

In *Political Liberalism*, Rawls states that *political* situations appropriate to the use of a common notion of moral personality and two moral powers are "those involving what we may call 'constitutional essentials' and questions of basic justice" (214). Constitutional essentials can be further divided into two broad categories: those

> (a) which specify the general structure of government and the political process and the essentials under (b) which specify the equal basic rights and liberties of citizens. Essentials of the first kind can be specified in various ways. Witness the difference between presidential and cabinet government. . . . By contrast, the essentials of the second kind concern basic rights and liberties and can be specified in but one way, modulo relatively small variations. Liberty of conscience and freedom of association, and the political rights of freedom of speech, voting and running for office are characterized in more or less the same manner in all free regimes (214).

Some might immediately undermine the neatness of constitutional essentials by identifying more ambiguous topics for review. Rawls anticipates the response. Some might consider "tax legislation and many laws regulating property; statutes protecting the environment and controlling pollution; establishing national parks and preserving wilderness areas and animal and plant species; and laying aside funds for museums and the arts" as "political concerns," Rawls acknowledges. But these differ from necessary constitutional essentials; they do not ask us to occupy our roles as citizens; they "do not concern those fundamental matters" related to basic liberties Rawls will claim (214). We might call them political but nonessential concerns.

Moreover, some will note how the varied elements of justice, particularly those associated with distributive matters, create doubts about where to draw (intra-constitutional essential) bounds. About these Rawls simply states that

> while some principle of opportunity is surely such an essential, for example, a principle requiring at least freedom of movement and free choice of occupation, fair equality of opportunity (as I have specified it) goes beyond that and is not such an essential. Similarly, though a social minimum providing for the basic needs of all citizens is also an essential, what I have called the 'difference principle' is more demanding and is not (228-29).

The strong demands of pluralism cannot allow our notion of personhood to be exercised or imposed upon with respect to every concern. More specifically, the difference principle falls short of being a core concern because

> whether the aims of the principles covering social and economic inequalities are realized is far more difficult to ascertain. These matters are nearly always open to wide differences of reasonable opinion; they rest on complicated inferences and intuitive judgments that require us to assess complex social and economic information about topics poorly understood . . . we can expect more agreement about whether the principles for the basic rights and liberties are realized than about whether the principles for social and economic justice are realized (230-31).

Constitutional essentials are "urgent" matters and more easily agreed upon within a liberal democracy (230).

But there is more to consider than this public and private distinction. A convincing political liberalism defends its assumptions about free and equal personhood by claiming that such moral requirements are not even Kantian. Political liberalism calls them freestanding, "political not metaphysical." This means that discussions about "moral personality" emerge as we "collect such settled convictions as the belief in religious toleration and the rejection of slavery and try to organize the basic ideas and principles implicit in these convictions" (8). Our equal status and shared understandings are not associated with comprehensive assumptions (Kantian, Millian, or otherwise) but with "the public culture itself as the shared fund of implicitly recognized basic ideas and principles" (8). Rawls adds that his is "not a psychology originating in the science of human nature but rather a scheme of concepts and principles for expressing a certain political conception of the person and an ideal of citizenship" (86-7). Full autonomy is a (minimally) moral expectation for citizens thinking about and acting on equality under "reasonable" restrictions (such as those established to situate them equally and allow them to establish fair public principles). It is "modeled by the structural aspects of the original position" (including its demand to don a veil of ignorance) and "achieved by citizens" and "realized in public life by affirming the political principles of justice" (77). This must be distinguished from "ethical autonomy" which "may apply to the whole of life." "[T]he weight of ethical autonomy [is] to be decided by citizens severally in light of their comprehensive doctrines" (78).

Finally, moral assumptions in political liberalism remain culturally specific. Perhaps we can articulate something about the dignity of all people, but in general, applying our moral expectations about persons to all societies, "hierarchical" or liberal (Rawls 1993) remains suspect. Most models for a political notion of the person drawn from western thought need to be acknowledged as such.

Historicism becomes a key starting point for Rawls. Certain moral assumptions are "fixed" "social facts" and considered convictions about moral personality are discovered as the "inevitable outcome of public reason" (1993, 37). They are endorsed by a reasonable range of diverse individuals living in our culture. Such moral assumptions never become "neutral" in the sense of being derived from a totally independent moral order. But they provide the content for a near-neutral conception of the person (or as close as we are likely to get) given their widespread acceptance and history.

One might launch an internal critique of Rawls complaining that significant Kantian (hence metaphysical) elements lurk here. Too many ambiguous references to Kant remain tucked away in footnotes throughout *Political Liberalism*,[4] too many analogous structural features of Kantian ethics just happen to shape the historically derived "fundamental ideas" grounding justice as fairness and its notion of moral personality.[5] I will review a few such problems. But to focus on this has difficulties. Kant did not direct his notion of moral autonomy and reason toward such limited issues; his position relied on a free self that Rawls has worked hard to avoid;[6] and certainly Kant would not ground practical reason on shared beliefs or "plain truths" from our culture. Kantians might remind us that the *Groundwork* (1964) does start from an explication of "common sense" morality and our intuitive shared understandings about right and wrong before talking about any higher moral imperative. But, while the phenomenal world might confirm the unarticulated, everyday use of autonomy and the categorical imperative or universalizing, for Kant the proper demands of practical reason and moral worth never flow from everyday life or "our political culture."

However, specific tensions do remain in a theory so dependent on a rigid distinction between political essentials and nonessentials, and between these and other "nonpolitical" concerns. There is also the problem of political liberalism's reading of history as one stable narrative about our culture. Rawls's use of history may only re-echo communitarian (often neo-Hegelian) visions (Schwartenbach 1991). Finally, the desire to limit the universal tendencies of liberal moral assumptions looks suspect, especially when Rawls (and others like Bruce Ackerman) have hoped to use those ideas to confirm a "law of peoples" (1993). With such confusions and vacillations the "political" character of this project gets unsettled. The result is doubt about how well political liberalism fosters the most generous arrangement for sustaining an abstract notion of equality alongside a robust level of moral diversity.

Rethinking the Limited Scope Requirement

For political liberalism, a "reasonable moral psychology" transcends our differences and legitimately describes us as equals only when its demands are limited to acts such as voting, deliberating about public laws, interpreting constitutional essentials and the like. Insisting upon such a capacity to understand public (or political) roles in contrast to nonpublic (or nonpolitical) ones is not altogether untenable or undesirable. We do act differently in churches and civic associations compared to government legislatures, courts, and a host of other "public" institutions. However, the "public" realm is not always (nor should it be) so set or stable; and Rawls himself voices deep equivocations about keeping the political essential vs. nonessential distinction in tact.

For example, when first introducing "constitutional essentials" Rawls backs away from specifics by writing the following:

> Many if not most political questions do not concern those fundamental matters (or constitutional essentials), for example much tax legislation and many laws regulating property; statutes protecting the environment and controlling pollution; establishing national parks and preserving wilderness areas and animal and plant species; and laying aside funds for museums and the arts. Of course, sometimes these do involve fundamental matters. A full account of public reason would take up these other questions and explain in more detail than I can here how they differ from constitutional essentials and questions of basic justice and why the restrictions imposed by public reason may not apply to them; or if they do, not in the same way, or so strictly (214-15).

Is this possible slippage between political essential and nonessential concerns good enough? How can it stand without further explanation?

Rawls moves on to clarify political essential vs. nonessential concerns through a distinction, noted above, between basic liberties and a social minimum. But do public essentials only include basic liberties? Are "the aims of the principles covering social and economic inequalities" so much more "difficult to ascertain," so much more "open to wide differences of reasonable opinion"

Perhaps. But Rawls thinks we agree to his egalitarian difference principle in an original position. Moreover, he says at one (all too brief) point at the outset of *Political Liberalism* that "the first principle covering the equal basic rights and liberties may easily be preceded by a lexically prior principle requiring that citizens' basic needs be met, at least insofar as their being met is necessary for citizens to understand and to be able fruitfully to exercise those rights and liberties. Certainly any such principle must be assumed in applying the first principle" (7). But how to assess such basic needs without reference to more complex economic considerations? Note too Rawls's confidence (in "The Basic Liberties and their Priorities") about rejecting the U.S. Supreme Court's decision to undermine public financing of political campaigns (359). Here we are assured that Rawls can discuss a complex and highly controversial economic policy question.

Rawls leaves himself open to questions then. But so far only the distinction between constitutional essentials and other political nonessentials has been mentioned. Perhaps political liberalism does a better job distinguishing between our roles and activities in political vs. nonpolitical settings. Yet recall that Rawls draws his political/nonpolitical (political vs. comprehensive moral) distinction from our democratic "culture." How can a background culture ensure such understandings? If it can, does this imply that civic associations (with nonpolitical demands) must educate their members in order to generate the proper understanding of citizenship? If education is required, aren't Rawls's strict distinctions and limited scope demand confounded?

The problem of how to educate good citizens, as Rousseau noted centuries ago, is fundamental to good democracy; yet it generates a paradox: "Each individual, appreciating no other aspect of government than the one that relates to his private interest, has difficulty perceiving the advantages he should obtain from the continual deprivations imposed by good laws. In order for an emerging people to appreciate the healthy maxims of politics, and follow the fundamental rules of statecraft, the effect would have to become the cause; the social spirit, which should be the result of the institution, would have to preside over the founding of the institution itself; and men would have to be prior to laws what they ought to become by means of laws" (Rousseau 1987, II, vii). Rawls tries to get around Rousseau's paradox by claiming that the "fundamental" ideas of democratic culture—including the core (moral) characteristics of moral personality for citizenship—emerge from "our history." For the most part, the need to "educate" goes unmentioned.

Yet Rawls does write at one point that strictly political institutions and their representatives (like the supreme court and its judges) should "educate" citizens by example (239-40). And elsewhere, hints surface via references to Rousseau. In an important footnote evoking *Emile*, Rawls discusses the kind of trust political liberals should have in fellow citizens whose moral personality must exhibit "evident intention to strive to do their part in just and fair arrangements" (86). Rawls also cites *On the Social Contract* when discussing how citizens should

understand the relation between their public and private interests.[7] It would seem
that Rawls wants citizens to understand just where a private perspective ends
and a public viewpoint begins. But again, having cited Rousseau, Rawls offers
little follow up on the broader lessons from Rousseau. The latter at least acknowledged education's central role in generating proper political sensibilities.
To ignore these points may make one's moral assumptions appear stable, perhaps strictly limited in scope, but they may also look unreasonable.

To his credit, Rawls anticipates some such problems too—or at least how his
distinctions may fail to find ideal expression (assuming that education will not
be a major part of his theory). For example, at one point in "The Idea of Public
Reason" Rawls acknowledges the intensity of democratic struggles over the
interpretation of constitutional essentials. In these cases, politics and the role of
citizenship are less clearly delineated, perhaps up for reevaluation.

Take for example political situations where individuals argue over what it
means to provide "fair equality of opportunity as it applies to education for all."
We might find, Rawls admits, that here "[d]iverse religious groups oppose one
another, one group favoring government support for public education alone,
another group favoring government support for church schools as well. The first
group views the latter policy as incompatible with the so-called separation of
church and state, whereas the second denies this. In this situation those of different faiths may come to doubt the sincerity of one another's allegiance to fundamental political values" (248). True enough. So how to deal with the muddle
made of the political essentials/political nonessential distinction in these cases?
Rawls continues:

> One way this doubt (about the sincerity of one's opponents) might be put to
> rest is for the leaders of the opposing groups to present in the public forum how
> their comprehensive doctrines do indeed affirm those values (the fundamental
> political ones). Of course, it is already part of the background culture to exam-
> ine how various doctrines support, or fail to support, the political conception.
> But in the present kind of case, should the recognized leaders affirm that fact in
> the public forum, their doing so may help to show that the overlapping consen-
> sus is not a mere modus vivendi. This knowledge surely strengthens mutual
> trust and public confidence; it can be a vital part of the sociological basis en-
> couraging citizens to honor the ideal of public reason (249).

Rawls's admission is important. But will religious doctrines neatly confirm
"the political conception" and our common understanding of how citizens
should be viewed as free and equal? Laying out more consistent articulations of
how comprehensive views may support various interpretations may indeed happen when we are acting in public. But this may show all the more reason to dis-
trust or acknowledge how foreign (especially some religiously inspired) views
feel from others. (Think of debates over teaching evolution or creationism in
public schools.) Certain debates do not necessarily lead to a strong stable consensus and respect for others qua citizens.

Establishing strong public/nonpublic distinctions can promote unfair consequences as well. Certain political/domestic, moral/legal, public/private distinctions may look "essential" and worthwhile in protecting certain private "rights."
But they are/were likely to make certain identities less important; or undermine
the claims of some perspectives seemingly entitled to a public hearing. Keeping
domestic violence under wraps may not have been the only reason for the promotion of earlier boundaries between public/private domains. But it was one
consequence of a seemingly reasonable construction of personhood. What would
have occurred if past attempts to redefine certain private behavior as illegal had
to abide by all aspects of the well-entrenched domestic/political, private/public,
moral/legal distinctions as defined by the times?

Toward these concerns, Rawls also considers himself attentive. He admits
that fundamental arguments over constitutional essentials (such as those surrounding slavery in the 19th century) may confound his limited scope ideal.
Clearly 19th century debates in the United States over slavery saw religious,
economic and otherwise distinctive "comprehensive" views of the person
evoked in public conversation (249). But Rawls insists that one can show, in
hindsight, how most positions that we now see on the morally right side in this
debate tacitly appropriated a public/nonpublic distinction and ultimately worked
with a properly public notion of the person. Rawls explains this way:

> Did the abolitionists go against the ideal of public reason? Let us view
> the question conceptually and not historically, and take for granted that their
> political agitation was a necessary political force leading to the Civil War and
> so to the destruction of the great evil and curse of slavery. Surely they hoped
> for that result and they could have seen their actions as the best way to bring
> about a well-ordered and just society in which the ideal of public reason could
> eventually be honored. Similar questions can be raised about the leaders of the
> civil rights movement. The abolitionists and King would not have been unrea-
> sonable in these conjectured beliefs if the political forces they led were among
> the necessary historical conditions to establish political justice, as does indeed
> seem plausible in their situation.
>
> On this account the abolitionists and the leaders of the civil rights
> movement did not go against the ideal of public reason; or rather, they did not
> provided they thought, or on reflection would have thought (as they certainly
> could have thought), that the comprehensive reasons they appealed to were re-
> quired to give sufficient strength to the political conception to be subsequently
> realized (251).

Could a sense of what was public versus private reasoning have operated here
even if agents did not intend it or were unclear about its standing? Perhaps.
Rawls's own language especially in the second paragraph above, makes the idea
sound rather strained though. Moreover, imagine applying this idea to intractable moral debates today. Perhaps fifty years from now (after some kind of conservative religious revolution) most of us will believe that the merging of egg

and sperm breathes life into an agent with equal rights. Men and/or women choosing to violate those rights, to "murder" an embryo, would be imprisoned, in some cases fined. We might say, in that future, that the moral assumptions worthy of our support and necessary for us as citizens stood behind the arguments used by past anti-abortion activists. It simply required time before becoming apparent.

But would this make the case for how Rawls's notion of the person now remains attentive to oppression? Would it help ensure that any other present-day struggles would use a political sense of the self on behalf of the morally right (though later to be recognized as such) position? Rawls's passionate rejection of slavery is not at issue here. The problem is that a) it is never completely clear that Rawls's notion of the person as described can exist behind every difficult conflict even over essential political issues; nor is it ever completely clear that one would want it, unchallenged, to do so; and b) the attempt to solidify the limited scope of Rawls's moral assumptions by claiming that they will be used as an ever-critical, always available champion for the oppressed and the "right" side seems too easy to claim in hindsight.[8] Rawls's assurance about our ability to exercise citizenship within a strictly limited scope still seems placed on shaky ground.

The Ambiguity of "Political" vs. "Moral" Autonomy

What about the freestanding requirement of political liberalism? Political liberalism's "thin" assumptions about moral personality remain freestanding by avoiding comprehensive moral claims. Here's how: i. Rawls has an explicit characterization of desires and desire formation, reason and moral capacity that are notably noninstrumental but supposedly not linked to Kant (or any single controversial view of the self). In addition, ii. when trying to strike an important balance between viewing persons as self-interested selves (with their own rational life plans) and as capable of benevolent reciprocity leading to respect or impartial conduct (for purposes of thinking about justice and abiding by fair terms of cooperation), Rawls does not claim that his assumptions come from anything but our political culture and what it has taught us. Rawls refers in *Political Liberalism* to "full autonomy" as a capacity that all citizens can (and should) exercise when they agree to follow fair terms of justice. And iii. any mention of autonomy or freedom, just like any talk of moral psychology found throughout *Political Liberalism*, is said to be political, and is never demanded in our private roles.

I would argue that elements in ii. above are called into question in part by the concerns raised in the earlier section about our political culture. Points i. and iii. are slightly more distinctive, and Rawls gives them ample attention in order to make this freestanding requirement stick.

In *Political Liberalism* Rawls offers a new discussion of "the basis of moral motivation in the person." It describes in detail the way political liberalism now views desire-formation, reasoning, and moral capacities as nonmetaphysical and noncontroversial "for us." A look at these ideas proves telling.

In his lecture on "The Power of Citizens and their Representatives," Rawls discusses "a reasonable moral psychology" in order to explain "the desire to realize a political ideal of citizenship" or why we propose fair terms of cooperation and abide by such terms at all (82). This is a critical component of political liberalism's approach to moral personality. To make these ideas clear and assure us that he can fill in some details about moral psychology without lapsing into references to "human nature" (or repeating certain mistakes in part III of *Theory* (xix)), Rawls distinguishes between "three kinds of desires." We all have "object-dependent," "principle-dependent" and "conception-dependent desires," Rawls claims (82-84). On this account, object-dependent desires refer to lower-level urges that "can be described without the use of any moral conceptions, or reasonable or rational principles" (82). These include bodily desires, those for food and drink and sleep. They may also include "desires to engage in pleasurable activities of innumerable kinds as well as desires that depend on social life: desires for status, power and glory, and for property and wealth. Add to these attachments and affections, loyalties and devotions of many kinds, and desires to pursue certain vocations and to prepare oneself for them" (82).

Principle-dependent desires, by contrast, are "activities" modified by rational or reasonable principles. "Two kinds" of principle-dependent desires exist then. Desires may be shaped by our means-end reasoning and our interest in ordering and prioritizing our claims (the rational); or by our interest in conducting ourselves fairly in relation to others (the reasonable). Depending upon the expectations and situations guiding an agent, we can identify a range of principle-dependent desires (83).

Finally, there are conception-dependent desires, evident when "the principles we desire to act from are seen as belonging to, and as helping to articulate, a certain rational or reasonable conception or political ideal" (84). For example, we may wish to act from principle-dependent desires, as opposed to object-dependent desires "governed by custom and habit." But the former "must be suitably related to the conception in question. . . . To speak of our having conception-dependent desires we must be able to form the corresponding conception and to see how the principles belong to and help to articulate it" (84). The "main" conception-dependent desire for persons envisioned in Rawls's theory is "the ideal of citizenship as characterized in justice as fairness" (84).

Rawls sees these claims drawn from a scheme of concepts and principles developed for a certain purpose. He suggests no links to one, necessary moral psychology (87). But are Rawls's psychological facts so divorced from a moral doctrine?

In an odd footnote that tries to tackle this question, Rawls makes two points. The first tries to make sense of the higher-order, conception-dependent level of desires and reasoning, claiming that "we have only to suppose that Kant's idea of the categorical imperative is coherent and say that a person with a good will is someone effectively moved by the conception-dependent desire to act as that imperative requires" (85, n.33). Some desires (object-dependent) are seen as almost completely brute or unmodified. Others can be given more complex ordering (perhaps put into life plans—or maxims as a Kantian might put it). Still others finally reach a higher-order level, one that Rawls equates with being able to be motivated by Kant's notion of the good will. Moreover, Rawls says several times that his account differs notably from a Humean account of desires and reason.

In the same footnote paraphrased above, Rawls does say that he envisions his general assumptions about moral psychology to have become widespread via our public culture. But this is said in passing. To say more about how such a psychology becomes a part of our culture is a "long and different story," Rawls adds evasively. Citing his debts to an article by Christine Korsgaard, a well-known Kant scholar and defender of Kantian ideas, and drawing contrasts between Korsgaard and Bernard William's broadly Humean account of motivation, Rawls ends his comments in the above cited footnote. But one thing seems clear: the source for the account of moral motivation is quite clearly Kantian-inspired.

Are the Kantian elements noted just a coincidence of history? Kant just happens to articulate what "we" share at this point in time? How so when our history is said to be a "long story," the empirical details of which a political liberalism will not discuss? Indeed, one might speculate that the source for Rawls's notion of history is not far from an enlightenment ideal which envisioned the progress of Reason over time (and which Kant himself well appreciated[9]). If Rawls could offer a better account of how his historicism works, of how it helps really distance his work from Kant's, the footnote quoted might not seem so troublesome. Leaving things as they stand, Rawls prompts doubt, again, about the stability of another key requirement for political liberalism.

Many might note that the revised "Kantian Constructivism" lectures in *Political Liberalism*, now entitled "Political Constructivism," do a better job distinguishing Rawls from Kant. But even here, the demand for stability, for some foundation that explains why moral assumptions are particularly "fixed" for us, creates odd problems. In this lecture, Rawls's commitment to freestanding assumptions about moral personality depend upon a constructivist approach to political theory (90). This relates to our point ii. highlighted above. Drawing upon prominent ideas with consensus in our culture, we have a much more viable justification for assumptions about the person than philosophy or religion could provide. No doubt, Rawls admits in "Political Constructivism" that "history is full of surprises. We have to formulate an ideal of constitutional government to see whether it has force for us and can be put into practice successfully in the history of society" (87). But this is a risk we take in order to avoid the problems faced by theories dependent upon "truth" claims at the expense of ensuring toleration and attention to pluralism.

Yet Rawls does comment about "our history" here in ways that undermine this constructivism. For example, at one point, Rawls insists that the "social facts" and "fundamental ideas" used in the process of constructing just principles are not totally re-constructable. "No constructivist views, including Scanlon's, say that the facts that are relevant in practical reasoning and judgment are constructed, any more than they say that the conception of person and society are constructed" (121). But what exactly does this mean? The statement falls prior to a passage concerned to stabilize categories in order to ensure the rejection of slavery. As a result, it reads as understandable backpeddling given the desire to settle the immoral character of a heinous practice once and for all.

But the comment obviously marks an important problem as well. To quote Rawls more fully: "In claiming that slavery is unjust the relevant fact about it is not when it arose historically, or even whether it is economically efficient, but that it allows some persons to own others as their property. That is a fact about slavery, already there, so to speak, independent of the principles of justice. The idea of constructing facts seems incoherent" (122). William Connolly quotes the same passages in his own comments about political liberalism, charging that while this effort to condemn slavery is understandable, the overall demand "to make social facts simple" does not stand up to scrutiny. The problem, as Connolly points out, is that

> the most relevant moral fact about slavery, to slaveholders and defenders, was that slaves did not count as full persons. They could accept the Rawlsian formula of fairness to persons while contesting its application to slavery. Rawls would say that they were simply wrong in this respect: his judgment fits the facts while slaveholders misinterpreted them. But in leaving matters here Rawls again underplays the ethical importance of the dense network of culturally defined differences between the personhood of particular constituencies and numerous afflictions, inferiorities, liabilities, disorders, and defects attached to many that fall below this threshold (1995a, 35-36).

What Rawls reveals, Connolly notes, is how this selectively asks constructivism to lock certain interpretations into place after time has past. Some situations might warrant this. But the task of deciding which is not always so easy.[10] And to imagine so may block the potential for changes that many hope will occur in order to imagine new just possibilities. Moreover, if Rawls expects certain facts—notably those associated with his view of persons as motivated by conception-dependent desires, full autonomy, reasonableness, and freedom—to be "there" for us, something else may be needed to secure such facts. That something may be a "moral doctrine" (like Kant's). It may be a progressive view of history (like Kant's and/or Hegel's). In either case, it remains difficult to see such stability flowing from the "strictly freestanding" foundation that Rawls believes political liberalism must maintain.

Cultural Specificity and the Law of Peoples

In 1993, as the first edition of *Political Liberalism* was published, we also received Rawls's article "The Law of Peoples." One liberal ally found this latter piece by Rawls, with its efforts to apply liberalism to international law thoroughly dispiriting, a clear erosion of the universal, emancipatory potential associated liberal commitments to seeing human beings' as equal and due respect (Ackerman 1994). I would claim, however, that Rawls's adherence to his cultural specificity demand and the limits of political liberalism are by no means reinforced clearly through this article. "The Law of Peoples" expects political constructivism's social contract arrangement to legitimate principles for governing international as well as domestic affairs. We are supposed to see political liberalism as historicist and culturally specific at one level; but this article boldly expects to apply the same form of liberalism to conflict resolutions between (ideal) liberal and nonliberal societies alike.

In making claims for justice beyond our borders, Rawls knows he faces difficulties. Again, the motivation for joining his social contract builds on a conception of the person fundamental "for us." How can nonliberal—or what Rawls calls "consultarian hierarchical"—societies adopt a liberal model dependent upon culturally specific claims about our two moral powers and justify a law of peoples?

First, political liberalism can extend its ideal assumptions to "well-ordered" hierarchical societies. And such assumptions, while not associated with the two moral powers, can be tied to certain understandings about justice, moral duty and motivation that most societies likely do demonstrate, Rawls's claims. Hierarchical societies, when "well-ordered," should be peaceful and nonagressive; guided by law and their own form of justice which imposes moral duties, remains consistent in its application, and takes dissent seriously; governed by political institutions where "a family of representative bodies, or other assemblies . . . look after the important interests of all elements of society" (1993, 62). It should also be able to justify certain "minimum rights to means of subsistence and security (the right to life), liberty (freedom from slavery, serfdom, and forced occupations) and (personal) property, as well as to formal equality as expressed by the rules of natural justice (for example, that similar cases be treated similarly)" (62). A well-ordered hierarchical society "respects basic human rights" (63).

From these claims, it follows that such societies will prove able to negotiate with liberal societies for a law of peoples and imagine themselves in an original position and behind a veil of ignorance. Hierarchical societies, then, can engage in the constructivist, justice-seeking process, but without changing their internal beliefs (they need not have to see autonomy and the moral demands on citizens exactly as we do). The original position and its requirements can apply to a second, general level more international rather than domestic in its goals. Of course, if a hierarchical society is tyrannical, dismissive of certain basic human rights, inattentive to internal dissent, it lacks the minimal capacity for reasonableness allowing symmetry and fair agreement in a higher-level application of the original position. But Rawls seems to imagine such cases as rare; and when they do exist, a modus vivendi can provide an alternative for reconciliation without violence.

This confident extension of political liberalism assumes that most societies, no matter what their internal political, social, or economic arrangements, "may still think their society should be treated equally in a just law of peoples, even though its members accept basic inequalities among themselves" (1993, 65). Moreover, the extension does not demand that fair equality of opportunity and a difference principle will result from these international efforts. Such aspects of justice as fairness may work for democratic societies like our own, but we rethink such outcomes when constructing principles for another purpose.

Unquestionably Rawls requires significant persuasive skills here. But as I see it, political liberalism must assume much more overlap between liberal and nonliberal societies, including their assumptions about what motivates persons, in order for a law of peoples to hold; otherwise the law of peoples applies to a more limited number of states than Rawls allows.

The main reason for these obvious comments goes back to the description of an ideal, well-ordered hierarchical society. Rawls expects members of the latter to readily enter an original position and imagine veiling their national character—"the size of the territory, or the population, or the relative strength of the people whose fundamental interests they represent" (1993, 54). The original position is pointless as a "device of representation" if this information, capable of thwarting cooperation, is well known. But Rawls has always said that entering the original positioning in good faith requires the capacity to exercise two moral powers. It is just not clear how the hierarchical society (or its representatives) engage in a hypothetical contract, even at this "second" more general level, unless liberal assumptions about personhood are fully entrenched beforehand.

Rawls suggests at another point that persons living in hierarchical societies need only exhibit rationality and reasonableness in their own way. By this, Rawls assumes "the parties care about the good of the society they represent, and so about its security as assured by the laws against war and aggression. They also care about the benefits of trade and assistance between peoples in times of need. . . . In view of this, we can say that the representatives of hierarchical societies are rational." Reasonableness means: "they do not try to extend their religious and philosophical doctrines to other peoples by war or aggression, and they respect the civic order and integrity of other societies" (1993, 64-65). Members of hierarchicals respect their moral duties. And, to repeat, those include a great deal: a willingness to remain nonexpansionist; respect for freedom of others and laws guided by justice; adoption of a court system with judges who address objections from members and who deal with them in good faith; rejection of religious persecution and full rights to emigration. This, and more, hierarchicals can sustain. But these look like a liberal society's expectations for its institutions and individuals. To my mind, Rawls has loaded much into the description of hierarchicals from the outset. Why wouldn't hierarchical societies entering an original position also have their representatives exercise autonomy in the full sense since they are expected to not only appreciate their sense of the good but to abstract from their particulars in order to aim for a higher-order sense of liberal justice? Rawls might say that he does make such a sweeping demand; but he asks it only of a "representative" of a hierarchical society, not all its members. But then isn't there a tremendous problem here with what constitutes a "people"?

Cultural specificity, as the final criteria for constructing a pluralism sensitive liberalism, looks strained by this article. "The Law of Peoples" looks to extend Rawls's notion of the person so that equality as he understands it becomes a model with cross-cultural potential, a universal model that may be called minimal, that may not lead to the second principle of justice, but that clearly remains reasonable for all humans. I may be sympathetic to this and its potential to support human rights. But if so, I would have to admit a willingness to (possibly) impose my ideas, to see them as necessarily higher-order or transcendent over the cultural configurations of many societies. This transcendence could not follow *after* we talk with all others at the negotiating table. Expectations for reasonableness will be well-established beforehand. Certain people will have to assimilate or stay out of the conversation. This approach may not lead to paternalism. But does it really look freestanding? Does it really lead to an ethic of mutual respect? What about the kind of respect we develop as a result of getting to know one another before demanding such weighty a priori expectations for what is just? We may indeed want certain other-regarding virtues exhibited during public negotiation. But Rawls's a priori expectations may still be too high, and the "Law of Peoples" may only reinforce this fear.

An important group of thinkers have drawn from political liberalism but adopted a different path for constructing and reevaluating equality given concern about pluralism. These include deliberative democrats such as Amy Gutmann and Dennis Thompson. For all their compatibility with Rawls, Gutmann and Thompson no longer support the Rawlsian conception of equal personhood, at least not in toto. They suggest that moral pluralism and recent concerns about conflict in liberal democracies require a new approach to who qualifies as an equal member of a flourishing democracy. Efforts like these merge somewhat with those articulated by thinkers like Seyla Benhabib and James Bohman. The latter forge a deliberative democratic characterization of equality and freedom in contrast to Jurgen Habermas's communicative ethic. Gutmann, Thompson, and others, recognize the vacillations and evasions of political liberalism. They hold onto our common capacity for autonomy, but without the same virtuous expectations for freedom that result in the original position. They do require citizens to exercise a set of virtues, but they consider these easily adopted, conducive to robust moral debate, and capable of demonstrating generosity toward different others. Deliberative democrats try to find a mutually legitimate new perspective from which to settle conflicts, and to overcome the moral incommensurability that they associate with multicultural liberal democracies like our own.

Notes

1. All parenthetical references to Rawls found in this paper are to the 1996 edition of *Political Liberalism* unless noted otherwise.

2. The liberal approach discussed here takes on a slightly different cast when interpreted through the writings of Bruce Ackerman or Charles Larmore. However, both see their ideas deeply indebted to Rawls's brand of political liberalism. Ackerman does remain concerned about Rawls's ongoing use of an original position; he also has reservations about Rawls's law of peoples (Ackerman 1994). In the past, Larmore had seemed to present an even more minimalist conception of personhood and equal respect (1987). But, in his later writings, more directly related to Rawls's work, few distinctions are drawn between his ideas and the ones discussed above from political liberalism (Larmore 1990). For the most part, I consider it safe to say that Rawls is the writer of towering influence in this model of liberalism. If the critique here has merit against him, those who follow his work closely face similar problems.

3. For another penetrating critique of political liberalism voicing similar reservations see Alejandro 1998, especially ch. 6.

4. See especially 1996, 25 n. 28; 48 n. 1; 51 n. 3; 82 n. 31; 93 n. 5; 102 n. 12; 120 n. 26; 207 n. 40; 213 n. 2.

5. See especially 1996, part I, i, sections 3-5; I, ii, sections 5-7.

6. See especially Rawls, 1996, 29-35.

7. Rawls writes: "On fundamental political questions the idea of public reason rejects common views of voting as a private and even personal matter. One view is that people may properly vote their preferences and interests, social and economic, not to mention their dislikes and hatreds. Democracy is said to be majority rule and a majority can do as it wishes. Another view, offhand quite different, is that people may vote what they see as right and true as their comprehensive convictions direct without taking into account public reasons.

Yet both views are similar in that neither recognizes the duty of civility and neither respects the limits of public reason in voting on matters of constitutional essentials and questions of basic justice. The first view is guided by our preferences and interests, the second view by what we see as the whole truth. Whereas public reason with its duty of civility gives a view about voting on fundamental questions in some ways reminiscent of Rousseau's *Social Contract*. He saw voting as ideally expressing our opinion as to which of the alternatives best advances the common good" (219-20).

8. William Connolly offers an important, closely related critique of Rawls in his "Suffering, Justice, and the Politics of Becoming" (1995a). Connolly reads Rawls as

unresponsive to the most formidable challenges within a democratic society that question settled identities and entrenched cultural determinations. The attempt to use slavery as an illustration of Rawls's capacity to attend to injustice is unconvincing. "Rawls is superb at acknowledging the justice of newly defined claims and constituencies once the politics of becoming has carried their voices within range of his hearing. And within a period of thirty years or so Rawlsians have acknowledged the claims of Indians, women and gays after a series of social movements began to reshape their cultural identifications. But Rawls pretends (and his categories presume) that he is in the same position with respect to a large variety of unpoliticized injuries today that he now is with respect to constituencies whose cultural identifications have been changed by the politics of becoming. And he also acts as if his own identity can remain untouched as he responds to such movements of difference." As Connolly sees it, "the point is not to criticize previous 'oversight' of Rawlsians, as if we have a clear view above the fray that they lack. . . . The point, rather, is to press Rawlsians to cultivate a bi-valent ethical sensibility responsive to the radical insufficiency of justice to itself. For it is extremely probable that all of us today are unattuned to some modes of suffering and exclusion that will have become ethically important tomorrow after a political movement carries them across the threshold of cultural attentiveness" (36-37).

9. See some of Kant's reflections on history (1985, 41-53; 176-90).

10. I should note that Connolly does not deny the attraction of a "neo-Hegelian" view of history. "Doesn't the trajectory of change in the shape of western universals reveal a historical dialectic filling the universal out progressively? Doesn't it show retrospectively that historically legitimate suffering imposed upon slaves, women, Indians, atheists and homosexuals was unjust or immoral? We can become neo-Hegelians. Indeed, it is very difficult not to from time to time. . . . And there is an ethical compulsion to treat the latest filling out of persons as the highest standard of personhood. It is just that this compulsion soon bumps into a discordant ethical imperative: to pursue practices of genealogy, deconstruction and political disturbance through which contemporary self-satisfied unities are rendered more problematical and more responsive to new movements of difference." (1995a, 39) I have not pursued this conclusion but remain "critically responsive" to it.

Chapter 3

Democratic Equality

Amy Gutmann and Dennis Thompson (1996), Seyla Benhabib (1992; 1994) and James Bohman (1995) represent a constellation of self-identified "deliberative democrats." They reconstruct equality around assumptions about our shared capacity for autonomy, but they emphasize links between autonomy and our capacities for self-legislation developed through interaction, interdependence, and dialogue with different "concrete others." This looks distinctive from the positions discussed thus far. It sidesteps key problems haunting Rawlsian liberalism and most notably the requirement that, as free and equal persons, citizens must transcend their differences in an abstract, isolated thought experiment. It sidesteps difficulties with Sen and Nussbaum who define us as humans able to translate differences through a list of common functioning capabilities. Deliberative democrats see our shared abilities bound up with the exercise of critical reflection and choice. But choice and reflection here require an openness toward information garnered in face-to-face dialogue and debate. The deliberative autonomy valued remains especially sensitive to a public hearing of diverse conceptions of the good. Only then will differences be appreciated. Only then will other-regarding sentiments like mutual respect follow. Respect flows from concrete struggle and debate with others whom we must get to know. Moreover, democratic "disharmony" may still result after differences are heard and "public" policies settled. This much deliberative democrats want to acknowledge and in so doing, make themselves more attentive than Rawls toward reevaluation of public principles for diverse democratic societies today.

Deliberative democrats do present a promising contrast. But they introduce their own deliberative dilemmas. Their expectations for autonomy and mutual respect also require exercise of "reciprocal recognition" toward others, a capacity that expects citizens to demonstrate a constellation of special characterological transformations. Not surprisingly, my comments below pose questions about such transformative demands. Do the latter serve as the reasonable prerequisites for joining a diverse democratic community?

While questioning deliberative democrats here, I do find their lessons instructive. However, the upshot of my observations suggests that deliberative democrats may appreciate and accommodate a "weak" version of moral pluralism, less so the "strong" level they hope for. This last point emerges more explicitly in chapter 4. Chapters 5 and 6 build on this idea and contrast the autonomy/respect positions discussed with agency/regard centered descriptions of our capacities qua free and equal persons. The autonomy/respect position, especially as associated with deliberative democrats, may be plausible and attractive when moral pluralism is desired; but an agency-oriented approach may function more effectively when differences and moral conflicts are especially robust. Before turning to these final points, this chapter outlines reasons for appreciating but qualifying the deliberative democratic ideal.

Describing Deliberative Democracy

Contrasts and Comparisons

Over the past decade, Amy Gutmann and Dennis Thompson have established the contours and applications of a deliberative democratic alternative. They carefully compare their ideas with others claiming that their brand of democracy offers "a broader, more political" approach to freedom and equality (Gutmann 1993b). This is the case because 1. significant problems exist with other forms of democracy, notably proceduralist (or populist) and constitutional (or Rawlsian liberal) in form; and 2. significant moral conflict never will be readily calculated away in our society, though it can be ameliorated legitimately through dynamic, interactive public forums.

Gutmann and Thompson sharpen their claims first through initial contrasts between procedural, constitutional, and deliberative democratic options. Such discussions are reviewed below with an eye toward revealing the deliberative democratic approach to free and equal personhood

As for "procedural democracy," Gutmann and Thompson claim that it offers one of the most popular ways to establish equality while resolving conflict fairly. Proceduralists count everyone's interests in relation to a formal procedure, such as voting. Individual interests expressed through the ballot balance respect for equality alongside efforts to resolve differences legitimately. The problem, however, is that proceduralists often do not link their views to any substantive moral conclusions. "Members of the losing minority can accept majoritarianism as a fair procedure," Gutmann and Thompson observe, "even when i yields incorrect results because it respects their status as political equals. The results of majority rule are legitimate because the procedure is fair, not because the results are right." In fact: "Some procedural democrats go further in their defense and deny that there are any correct substantive moral conclusions and politics" (1996, 28). Gutmann and Thompson respond by stating that "the defense of procedural democracy does not require this moral skepticism, and indeed it would undermine the defense. If there's no reason to believe that any moral claim is valid, then there's no reason to count anyone's moral claim at all, and no reason, therefore, to defer to the claims of the greatest number" (28). Proceduralists ultimately value a more weighty understanding of equality, but they refuse to discuss or defend it explicitly.

The issue becomes more pressing when procedural democrats admit that "the majority must respect politically relevant rights such as freedoms of speech, the press, and association, the rule of law, and universal adult suffrage" (31). As Gutmann and Thompson see it, such liberties and opportunities,

> which are (arguably) necessary conditions of a fair democratic process, are not valued only for this procedural reason. . . . Whether or not religious freedom, for example, is necessary for the democratic process, it remains a basic liberty of individuals and therefore a moral constraint on majority rule. . . . Just as proceduralism recognizes limits on majority rule in order to respect individuals as equal citizens, so it must also admit limits to protect basic liberty and opportunity in order to respect individuals as equal persons, each with his or her own life to lead (31).

The claim, then, is that proceduralists often have their own commitment to basic freedoms and cannot argue that the priority for democracy is simply majority rule. Although proceduralism tries "to make do with few substantive moral constraints, and neglect[s] the need for substantive moral discussion" this is not a feasible option (33). Commitments to basic freedoms presuppose acknowledgment of a core moral value. Proceduralists must acknowledge their implicit commitment to what Gutmann, in an earlier article, calls political autonomy "understood as self-government, the willingness and ability to shape one's private or public life through deliberation, informed reflection, evaluation, and persuasion that allies rhetoric to reason" (Gutmann 1993b, 140). Moreover, "to decide whether majority rule or some other procedure is justified, citizens have to deliberate about the substantive value of alternative procedures. . . . Proceduralists therefore need to incorporate deliberation as a precondition for adequately resolving political disputes about procedures" (Gutmann and Thompson 1996, 32). To describe us simply as persons with self-interested desires who deserve equal treatment within the context of a particular procedure is not enough. We must recognize ourselves as free in a very specific way.

Constitutional democracy, as represented by Rawls, might fare better. A hybrid democracy with commitments to a "positive" liberalism, this view shares distinct affinities with the autonomy-inspired foundation for deliberative democracy (Gutmann 1993b). Also, (liberal) democratic constitutionalists "give priority to some rights whose primary purpose is to produce justified outcomes by protecting the vital interests of individuals" (Gutmann and Thompson 1996, 34). But constitutionalists do not find favor either.

Rawls fails to emphasize enough of a link between autonomy as critical thinking and autonomy as argumentation about public issues. As Gutmann and Thompson put it,

> although [Rawls's] theory of constitutional democracy leaves room for such discussion, it emphasizes instead a solitary process of reflection, a kind of private deliberation. He [Rawls] suggests that each of us alone perform an intricate thought experiment in which a veil of ignorance obscures our own personal interests, including our conceptions of the good life, and compels us to judge on a more impersonal basis (37).

Rawls's assumptions about autonomy remain too abstract (and possibly Kantian); and, more importantly, the kind of solitary reflection Rawls finds compelling lacks the necessary generosity for listening and legitimately accommodating pluralism and its inevitable conflicts. Rawls does state that "even after we have gone through all the stages of thinking in the solitary process we're likely to find that 'this test (of solitary thinking) is often indeterminate.'" But deliberative democrats retort, "we must not check our deliberative dispositions at the door to the public forum" (38). At the point where things become indeterminate, we need collective efforts to interpret what to do. "Even if we cannot philosophically establish principles specific enough to determine justifiable policies, we should not dismiss the possibility of developing more conclusive moral reasons through public discussions in a process informed not only by the facts of political life but also by conceptions of the good life, and inspired by the ideals of deliberation" (39).

This suggests several other points. First, that the most viable assumptions about critical thinking and reasoning associated with justifying public principles should focus on how individuals can and should gather together different ideas and incorporate new, diverse perspectives into their own. Also, citizens should expect to exercise moral reflection that is participatory not only when talking about "constitutional essentials" but when debating in "middle democracy" (on issues related to schools, civic associations, and other local community institutions) (40). This should generate more active public exchanges and establish collective arrangements with authoritative standing. The deliberative democratic process, as contrasted with the Rawlsian original position, justifies its outcomes by taking seriously a wide range of moral perspectives.

As for strong social democrats like Nussbaum and Sen, Gutmann has responded indirectly to their approach. In a brief encyclopedia entry on democracy, she writes that for social democrats "the principled basis for democratization is typically not the intrinsic value of participation but rather avoidance of the tyrannical threat over individual lives that accompanies concentrations of power" (Gutmann 1993a, 416). Deliberative democrats do not completely dismiss such concerns, but they emphasize the "intrinsic value of participation" and deliberation, first and foremost. They remain wary, as well, of an assured, substantive approach to the common good, especially one that enables using a set list of needs never justified through ongoing deliberation. In addition, social democrats may not look skeptical enough about the way "too much state control threatens state tyranny" (416). At times, deliberative democrats arrive at conclusions much like social democrats; but the route they pursue will seem different. They expect their policy outcomes to look more legitimate given their initial emphasis on individual freedom.

But why does a more participatory notion of autonomy remain more accountable to pluralism? It incorporates civic virtues into its expectations about freedom and it expects to transform "incompatible values and incomplete understanding" thereby grounding public policies from a strongly moral and authoritative perspective. So do these ideas keep moral pluralism alive and well?

Participatory autonomy makes significant moral demands and Gutmann and Thompson identify these with a form of moral reasoning called "reciprocity." Reciprocity asks us to speak with civic "integrity" and "magnanimity," the latter promoting ways to acknowledge and remain open toward those with whom we disagree. Do such requests show less controversy than their counterparts? How do they remain "political" yet morally meaningful and generate "mutual" respect (as opposed to Rawlsian "abstract" respect) and "accommodation" (as opposed to transcendence or avoidance) of difference?

Equality and Reciprocity

Answering these questions requires analysis of democratic "reciprocity," a "leading principle" shaping the arguments here and establishing fair terms of social corporation (Gutmann and Thompson 1996, ch. 2).

Reciprocity establishes, first, obligations for how we should speak not what we should say. Second, it makes demands on others as it mitigates conflicts, but this is not unusual since we can expect fellow citizens to "share the goal of reaching deliberative agreement even when (they) disagree with one another's conclusions" (1996, 14). Third, deliberative democrats emphasize reciprocity's resistance to final, universal conclusions. It promotes "significant points of convergence (but not a consensus) between one's own understandings and those of citizens whose positions, taken in their more comprehensive forms, one must reject" (85). The aim of reciprocity

> is not necessarily to induce citizens to change their first-order moral beliefs. It is rather to encourage them to discover what aspects of those beliefs could be accepted as principled policies by other citizens with whom they fundamentally disagree. Since it is this second-order agreement that citizens should seek, they do not have to trade-off their personal moral views against public values. . . .

> This shift in focus of what democratic citizens should share is significant, theo-
> retically and practically. Theoretically, a deliberative perspective expresses as
> complete a conception of a common good as is possible within a morally plu-
> ralistic society. . . . Practically, this perspective encourages the cultivation of a
> set of civic virtues that can guide citizens through the maelstroms of moral con-
> troversy in a pluralistic society (93-94).

As for the first and second points, Gutmann and Thompson fill in the details by linking reciprocity to "mutual respect"; and the latter, in turn, "comprises a family of moral dispositions" (81). One set of reciprocity-oriented dispositions leading to respect relates to the expectations one places on oneself and the con-sistency of one's speech when forming moral arguments and expressing them publicly. These "call on citizens to affirm" "civic integrity." And such integrity is demonstrated "in three ways": i. "by consistency in speech" whereby indi-viduals demonstrate sincerity about the positions they hold and do not simply promote a position "for reasons of political advantage" (81); ii. by "consistency between speech and action" such that someone who promotes a particular point of view also acts in a way consistent with the views propounded in public; and iii. by "integrity of principle" whereby one accepts "the broader implications of the principles proposed by one's moral positions" (81-82).

Another set of dispositions focuses on "one's judgments of others" (82). These promote magnanimity in the following ways: i. They require acknowl-edgment of how an opponent's position will often be based on a moral "rather than a purely strategic, political, or economic view"; in other words, when speaking with others one should not immediately "impugn the moral status of an opponent's position" by implying that others are simply "politically motivated" (82-83). ii. They also demand that citizens remain "open minded" and "try to break personal and institutional habits that would discourage them from accept-ing an opposing position at some time in the future, or at least from modifying their position in that direction" (83). Coupled with openness, deliberative de-mocrats encourage "a commitment to finding a mutually acceptable value . . . that could help resolve moral differences at the level of policy. Ronald Dworkin invokes a related value—the sacredness of life—in a similar effort to find com-mon ground among adversaries in the abortion conflict." Finally i and ii should lead to iii. "what we call the economy of moral disagreement," something akin to efforts to make accommodations with others who are owed our reciprocity and, therefore, owed our willingness to minimize the range of public disagree-ment that exists between us (87-89).

Overall, reciprocity leading to mutual respect is unlike "abstract respect" since the former avoids an impartial construction of freedom and reason where citizens are asked to "suppress or disregard their partial perspective and individ-ual projects when making policies and laws" (54). Not only is an impartial char-acterization of reasoning leading to abstract respect unlikely, it is undesirable (52-62).

Deliberative Democracy and Discourse Ethics

Other prominent, self-described deliberative democrats include Habermasian-influenced figures such as Seyla Benhabib and James Bohman. The latter receive less attention here, but we should note that while these thinkers have revised discourse ethics in order to retain "the crucial insights of the universalist tradition in practical philosophy . . . without committing . . . to the metaphysical illusions of the Enlightenment" (Benhabib 1992, 4), they have associated themselves with formulations about autonomy that complement, if not overlap significantly with, Gutmann and Thompson's.

Benhabib's affinities, with Gutmann especially, emerge through a commitment to equality understood in relation to "modern theories of autonomy." For Benhabib, we envision ourselves as equals in relation to the exercise of "free consent." "The central insights of communicative or discourse ethics derives from modern theories of autonomy and of the social contract, as articulated by John Locke, and Jean-Jacques Rousseau, and in particular by Immanuel Kant. Only those norms and normative institutional arrangements are valid, it is claimed, which individuals can or would freely consent to as a result of engaging in certain argumentative practices" (Benhabib 1992, 24). These "argumentative practices" then adopt a distinctive character through insights from Karl-Otto Apel and Jurgen Habermas. "Such argumentative practices can be described as an 'ideal community of communication'" (24). The idea is to maintain the insights of the Kantian principle of universalizability and ethics but add a distinctly participatory component to the demands of autonomy. Habermas and others have taken seriously Hegel's critique of formalist and universalist ethical theories and integrated "lessons" about the "concrete historical-ethical community" (24) into a proceduralist model. A discourse ethic then sees the advantages to something like Rawls's original position, for example. But it tries to formulate autonomy as a device for interpersonal comparability less applicable in isolation and more as a test for public conversation.

> Instead of thinking of universalizability as a test of non-contradiction, we think of universalizability as a test of communicative agreements. We do not search for what would be non-self-contradictory but rather for what would be mutually acceptable for all. Furthermore, there is also a shift from the model of the goal-oriented or strategic action of a single agent intending a specific outcome to the model of communicative action which is speech and action to be shared with others (28).

Again, as Benhabib puts it: "Instead of asking what an individual moral agent could or would will, without self contradiction, to be a universal maxim for all, one asks: what norms or institutions would the members of an ideal or real communication community agree to as representing their common interests after engaging in a special kind of argumentation or conversation?" (28)

Although Rawls has gone some way toward diminishing links between autonomy and abstracting from our contexts behind the veil of ignorance (toward acknowledging a form of "public reason" and the importance of conversation), Benhabib has, nonetheless, discerned ambiguities in Rawls's latest efforts. If Rawls has now added a deliberative element to the universalizing process, he still fails to construct the "special kind of conversation" Benhabib applauds. Rawls restricts the agenda of public conversation too dramatically. He imagines deliberative rationality used only in the "legal sphere" and fails to see its full relevance in guiding actions in civil society, the latter understood in much the same manner as Gutmann and Thompson understand "middle democracy" (Benhabib 1994, 36-37).

In addition, Benhabib argues that Rawls fails to discuss in enough detail the virtues (or "strong ethical assumptions") associated with argumentative speech (1994; also 1992, 29). Again, like Gutmann and Thompson, Benhabib associates autonomy with the virtue of respect. But respect, as she understands it, does not demand detachment from life's particulars. Rather, a "principle of universal moral respect" requires i. "that we recognize the right of all beings capable of speech and action to be participants in the moral conversation" and it requires ii. "the principle of egalitarian reciprocity," namely "that within such conversations each has the same symmetrical rights to various speech acts, to initiate new topics, to ask for reflection about the presuppositions of the conversation" (1992, 29). Respect corresponds to "the 'golden rule'" with its emphasis on efforts to "judge from the point of view of others." But in its democratic form it requires a) acquisition of a "moral feeling . . . through . . . processes of communicative socialization" plus b) active engagement with concrete others in a struggle to listen, "recognize" and eventually understand them as different, and c) acknowledgment that such substantive presuppositions can be bracketed and reassessed at some point (although the burden is on challengers to demonstrate why such presuppositions are not valid) (32). As "reciprocal recognition," the latter reinforces how "without engagement, confrontation, dialogue and even a 'struggle for recognition' in the Hegelian sense, we tend to constitute the otherness of the other by projection and fantasy or ignore it in indifference" (168). "In conversation, I must know how to listen, I must know how to understand your point of view, I must learn to represent it to myself" (52).

In short, Benhabib refuses to emphasize simply our need for freedom from interference. "Positive" freedom to do or be a certain way is part of who we are and worth striving for. Such freedom, as autonomy, works only through collective deliberation. And such deliberation must occur through demonstrations of concrete mutual respect with expectations for openness and understanding that generate legitimate agreement.

Moreover, like Gutmann and Thompson, this Habermasian strain of deliberative democracy establishes its position in contrast with Rawlsian liberalism and democratic majoritarians. As for Rawls, he should modify his neo-Kantian-like proceduralist vision while adding substantive and expansive elements to the practice of autonomy. As for majoritarians, Benhabib follows Gutmann and Thompson, writing that:

in many instances majority rule is a fair and rational decision procedure, not because legitimacy resides in numbers, but because if a majority of people are convinced at one point in time on the basis of reasons formulated as closely as possible as a result of a process of discursive deliberation that conclusion 'A' is the right thing to do, then this conclusion can remain valid. . . . It is not the sheer numbers which support the rationality of the conclusion, but the presumption that if a large number of people see certain matters in a certain way as a result of following certain kinds of rational procedures of deliberation . . . then such a conclusion has a presumptive claim to being rational until shown to be otherwise (1994, 33).

Finally, Benhabib, claims to present a particularly generous approach to pluralism. If and when we face moral conflict, similarities should not assimilate differences by abstracting from our situations and imagining an archetypical single point of view. Nor should we displace our particular needs and find common ground based on a fully developed scale of universal common goods (or natural needs). We construct a level of civility to deliberate about what we share and use a procedure to "keep the conversation going" (1994, 32) within limits even as we aim to transform and accommodate conflict though positive "mutual understanding of otherness" (1992, 168).

Deliberative Dilemmas

In short, deliberative democrats expect two main things from autonomous speakers: dispositions related to the way individuals view their own speech in public and dispositions related to the way individuals make judgments about what others have to say. The first, identified by Gutmann and Thompson as "civic integrity," asks for a willingness to speak in public in ways that show sincerity, not just an instrumental set of concerns, as well as consistency and long-term critical thinking about the implications of a position taken. The second, related to "civic magnanimity," requests generous openness toward positions unlike our own. True, moral pluralism deeply limits how much we can know about others. As Gutmann and Thompson put it "the persistence of moral disagreement" leads to "incompatible value" and "incomplete understanding" (1996, 24-25). But these formal requests that demonstrate magnanimity marked by openness, sometimes referred to as "open-mindedness," are critical to the reciprocity that helps us treat others fairly, bridge differences without abandoning "first order moral values," and avoid initially depending upon a uniform set of goods or needs for interpersonal comparability.

Having said this, most all deliberative democrats also suggest that their conceptions of freedom and mutual respect do more than promote toleration and simple coexistence. Nevertheless "democratic disharmony" remains too. "We reach some resolutions, but they are partial and tentative. The resolutions do not stand outside the process of moral argument, prior to it or protected from its provocations." "If incompatible values and incomplete understanding are as endemic to human politics as scarcity and the limited generosity, then the problem of moral disagreement is a condition with which we must learn to live, not merely an obstacle to be overcome on the way to a just society" (1996, 25-26).

This said, deliberative disharmony presents some special problems. Gutmann and Thompson, along with their counterparts, have a difficult time reaching for "second order" agreements that do not ask citizens to trade-off "first order" personal "moral views against public values" (1996, 93-94). This leads to more harmony or convergence than expected, and hence to serious questions about how far deliberative democrats can go toward accommodating the conflicts they expect democracy to produce.

The main problem here stems from expectations about reciprocity. When faced with moral conflicts based on "incompatible values" and "incomplete understanding" one might expect reciprocal openness to presuppose a chastened level of understanding about others, leading to a willingness to listen, to acknowledge others, and to keep a certain kind of conversation going. Instead, deliberative democratic reciprocity vacillates between what I would call a demand for open-mindedness and the more robust requirements of transformative openness whereby citizens use dialogue to reshape the clashes of first-order beliefs into a higher-order, newly synthesized third set of understandings. That third set is expected to emerge after the clash between different others leads to significant recognition and deeper compatibility with positions opposed. As differences dissipate, individuals seen as adversaries become partners in the process of mutual self-enlightenment. Questioned here is the deliberative democratic characterizations of the moral but supposedly undemanding virtue of magnanimous openness in particular. If reciprocity is bound up with openness and a fuller transformation through the medium of deliberation, it creates problems for properly accommodating pluralism based on "incomplete understanding." Transformation of the kind suggested may be desirable at times but should it remain the only option we have if assimilation is to be avoided?

Along with this first issue, I would claim that serious vacillations exist around democratic disharmony. This condition appears critical to preserving moral pluralism. It makes sure that a democratic polity aims toward "ongoing deliberative agreement" coupled with "disagreement" (Gutmann and Thompson 1996, 53), toward recognizing how "the political agenda is never likely to be free of fundamental moral conflict," and how we must learn to live with the possible intensification of moral conflict, possibly even an "ironic" stance toward final collective decisions (Benhabib 1992, 256). But throughout Gutmann and Thompson's work, we find few indeterminate policy decisions discussed, and rather sanguine expectations about the establishment of public policies resting on reconciled values. Autonomy may be distanced from its associations with Rawls's requirements and deliberation may aim for a more intelligible notion of respect alongside awareness that democracy has "remainders." However, lack of clarity produces questions about whether deliberative reciprocity can retain such full appreciation for the diversity it cherishes.

Open-mindedness and Transformative Openness

One way to explore the possible difficulties here is through a distinction between open-mindedness and transformative openness. In spirit, deliberative democrats commit to open-mindedness in order to sustain their distinctly formal virtues for citizens and their appreciation for moral pluralism. But when they move to the application of their ideas, they tend toward a transformative notion of openness. The latter underlies difficulties that prompt my questions about how well deliberative democrats create room for civil dissent from authoritative norms.

Deliberative democrats often claim that their expectations for openness are best demonstrated by exemplary individuals, statespersons and judges and perhaps moral philosophers, who have shown great willingness to listen to those with whom they disagree. Gutmann and Thompson offer their readers well chosen comments from politicians like former Congressman Bill Green and former governor Mario Cuomo, both of whom have favored aspects of the pro-choice position but have shown what they consider tremendous civic virtue through acknowledgment of, even expressed appreciation for, opponents. From Green's congressional speeches in the late 1980s, specifically responding to pro-life opponents, they highlight the following quotes:

> Let me at the outset say that I understand the depth of feeling of those who support the motion (to deny government funding for abortions in the case of rape and incest) and who feel that abortion should be permitted only when the life of the mother is in danger. I understand the sincerity with which those who advocate that position come to the floor. . . . Now, I know that obviously (our) position (in favor of funding abortions in cases of rape and incest) is one that is morally inconsistent with the position of those who are supporting the motion, but I suggest to you it is certainly an understandable, defensible position, and one which I would hope those who do not like abortion would nonetheless understand . . . I would hope that they would at least acknowledge that there is . . . moral controversy (Gutmann and Thompson 1996, 79).

Gutmann and Thompson cite Cuomo's public pronouncements about remaining pro-choice but also "eager for enlightenment, eager to learn new and better ways to manifest respect for the deep reverence for life that is our religion and our instinct." Even beyond this, there is a "hope that the public attempt to describe the problems as I understand them will give impetus to the dialogue in the Catholic community and beyond, a dialogue which could show me a better wisdom than I've been able to find so far" (1996, 81).

These examples do demonstrate open-mindedness manifest as thoughtful civil acknowledgment of an opponent's position. An opponent is neither slandered nor ignored here; presumably the response is sincere; more is at work than toleration since speakers are not simply putting up with those whom they disdain. There is also an effort to encourage speakers to witness and acknowledge others, to keep conversation going. And the possibility of cooperation or compromise exists, even if it is not yet reached. Finally, the examples show how magnanimous openness toward others may not be simply a theoretical projection. The attitude looks familiar; it encompasses what many believe can and does happen when we engage in public discourse at its best.

However, deliberative democracy has an inclination to go beyond the above and discuss further expectations. James Bohman, working from the vantage point of discourse ethics, claims that democratic equality describes a "regulative ideal" of citizenship that must encourage each individual on either side in a serious moral debate to "recognize (him/herself) in the mutual interpretations and criticisms" of others (Bohman 1995, 271). Like Gutmann and Thompson, he cites Ronald Dworkin's *Life's Dominion* as exemplary for rethinking common ground on the abortion controversy and suggests looking to promote openness that leads toward "a weak plural agreement, to which each side (in this or any moral controversy) could assent for different reasons" (269).

In relation to the abortion debate, Ronald Dworkin proposes adopting a framework in which the intrinsic value of human life is recognized as a deep and abiding shared understanding consistent with the "pro-life" perspective and with acknowledgment of the "procreative autonomy" of women. Dworkin does not see the fetus as a person with rights and interests to be protected against those of a woman. He argues strongly in favor of Blackmun's decision in *Roe v. Wade* (Dworkin 1993, 106-107). However, he wants to make sense of the vague language in Roe claiming that at some point in pregnancy a compelling state interest exists to protect human life. What shared intuition supports this? Dworkin answers:

> that human life has an intrinsic, innate human value; that human life is sacred just in itself; and that the sacred nature of a human life begins when its biological life begins, even before the creature whose life it is has movement or sensation or interests or rights of its own. According to (this) second claim (which is more compelling, and does not try to claim that a fetus has rights), abortion is wrong in principle because it disregards and insults the intrinsic value, the sacred character, of any stage or form of human life. I shall call this the detached objection to abortion, because it does not depend on or presuppose any particular rights or interest. Someone who accepts this objection, and argues that abortion should be prohibited or regulated by law for this reason, believes that government has a detached responsibility for protecting the intrinsic value of life (11).

Deliberative democrats may support such common ground as they reach for a new language to solidify agreements. The "sanctity principle" that Dworkin develops from this "detached objection" does not prohibit abortion. It acknowledges that "any human creature, including the most immature embryo, is a triumph of design or evolutionary creation, which produces a complex, reasoning being from, as it were, nothing." Such a shared framework provides a complicated explanation for why abortion in some cases is reasonable but in other cases more troubling. Since human life follows

> a certain natural course . . . it is a waste of the natural human and creative investments that make the story of a normal human life when this normal progression is frustrated by premature death or in other ways. But how bad this is —how great the frustration—depends on the stage of life in which it occurs, because the frustration is greater if it takes place after rather than before the person has made a significant personal investment in his own life, and less if it occurs after any investment has been substantially fulfilled, or as substantially fulfilled as is anyway likely (Dworkin 1993, 87-88).

The implication, of course, is that concerns over the later stages of gestation and many peoples' "frustration" against late term abortion can still be taken into account, and so too states' willingness to allow for abortion of deformed fetuses. All these approaches are actually incorporated into our laws. And this is because most people prefer thinking through this problem within a framework that takes the sanctity principal seriously based on the intrinsic value of life coupled with the standard investment measure of when life is more valuable.

Again, deliberative democracy can support this as a model because democratic moral compromise should not modify first-order differences to achieve unity (although it may when conflicts lack a certain depth). Rather, we modify conflicting interpretations of the existing framework so as to form a new framework where each can recognize the other's values (Bohman 1995, 268-69). Dworkin's proposals look especially attractive because they reach out to both sides in the abortion controversy. Both, Bohman writes,

> can find their moral reasons represented, interpreted, and assessed. It is far from the neutrality of the method of avoidance: citizens' values and conceptions of the good life are put up for public debate. The method of avoidance in this case does not promote public deliberation, but produces communities in which there is a wider and wider discrepancy in their interpretations of the framework and standards of evaluation. Similarly, this solution does not depend on overlapping consensus of antecedent values, but would depend upon the construction of a new and expanded framework for deliberating about differences (269).

Dworkin then provides a way of thinking such that "the compromise reached genuinely fuses together the existing frameworks (on different sides of the abortion debate) and thus modifies both of them. The parties will accept the new framework for different moral reasons, in light of how common deliberation and dialogue with the conflicting view has changed their original beliefs." Bohman continues, "Charles Taylor and others have argued that this is the structure of all inter-cultural understanding and comparative judgments. But in this case the transformation in moral beliefs and standards of justification is not merely generally broadening the horizon of understanding, but a deliberative process of reflection on each pair of conflicting values and beliefs and of the construction of a third, alternative set" (270).

But have we just read a description of open-mindedness leading to ongoing conversation and experimental efforts toward tentative agreement? If using the above as a guide for dealing with seemingly intractable differences, deliberative democracy presupposes that dialogue will necessarily forge deeper understandings and a new language for bridging differences. Of course, many who support abortion rights will ask whether they need to (or can) in a deep way—in a way that transforms, even if it does not transcend their particular experiences—understand the men and women whose identities are bound up with a tradition they have not experienced, who live, perhaps, in a part of the country they have never visited, who believe that women's role in society is misguided if it takes shape outside domestic work and child rearing, and in opposition to certain religious views. Some may welcome elements of a pro-life position into a public policy initiative and may wish to engage in negotiations about abortion policy. But deliberative democrats who reach for what Bohman discusses place their commitments to equality in a more demanding position. Can or should a sense of equality based on our shared need for freedom—and even fairness—always require that we review (and reveal) our deepest reasons and self-understandings in order to reach a higher plateau where mutual convergence becomes the only safe way to accommodate difference?

Open-mindedness manifest as a willingness to listen and acknowledge others makes sense—and makes good sense as a request from citizens who wish to participate in public debate that looks to mitigate (especially violent) conflict. But a Dworkin-like approach, as understood by Bohman here, shows that deliberative democrats may slide from open-mindedness toward an imperative for transformative encounters leading to reconciliation and convergence that do more than keep the conversation going and build exploratory coalitions. Little tentative talk occurs as the above model reaches for well-grounded solutions. Again, such results may appeal; but it remains less clear how deliberative democracy accommodates differences based on "a weak plural agreement to which each side could assent for different reasons" (Bohman 1995, 269).

We should return to Gutmann and Thompson and acknowledge that they may see potential difficulties here. They hesitate to endorse fully the kind of openness I draw out of Bohman. At times, they question efforts like Dworkin's. Gutmann and Thompson feel unclear about whether Dworkin will really allow both sides in the abortion debate to "see themselves" and their ideas given fair expression. In fact, from their vantage point, Dworkin starts off too assured about the pro-choice position: "If Dworkin could show that this claim (that human beings cannot have constitutional rights unless they have prior sentience or consciousness) is justifiable to pro-life as well as pro-choice advocates, then he would indeed resolve the controversy—and on terms that are consistent with the principle of reciprocity. But he does not succeed in defending this claim on mutually justifiable grounds" (Gutmann and Thompson 1996, 76). Gutmann and Thompson hope that their variation of deliberative democracy and reciprocal recognition is less quick to transform diversity; and when it does bridge differences, negotiation must keep going. Again, openness should occur not "to induce citizens to change their first-order moral beliefs . . . rather to encourage them to discover what aspects of those beliefs could be accepted as principled policies . . . (leading to a) second-order agreement (where citizens) . . . do not have to trade-off their personal moral views against public values" (93).

The problem, however, is that Gutmann and Thompson chastise Dworkin but immediately move to the following: everything we need to accommodate both sides in the abortion debate lies within the *Roe v. Wade* decision itself. We do not need Dworkin because we need only look to the Supreme Court and other majority decisions like the one in *Planned Parenthood vs. Casey* to find strategies for mutual justification. Add to the Court decisions further creative public policy initiatives respecting both sides in the debate and we can see reciprocity cultivated appropriately.

To be more specific, Gutmann and Thompson believe *Roe* demonstrates "open-mindedness" by balancing a pro-life and pro-choice position and giving both sides a significant say in final policy making.

> Although the court did not admit as a constitutional argument the claim that fetuses are persons, the majority opinion emphasized that the state has an interest in protecting potential life. This emphasis moved the rationale for the decision closer to the conclusions of a pro-life position, particularly as they applied to later stages of fetal development. Moreover, the court shifted the emphasis in this way without abandoning the premise that fetuses are not constitutional persons. The court allowed states to ban abortion in the third trimester, on the grounds that state interest in the potential life is compelling once the fetus is viable. On this logic, if medical technology advances and viability extends to earlier stages of pregnancy, then the court rationale should give increasing protections to fetal life (86).

Without drawing further contrasts between this point and their criticisms of Dworkin, Gutmann and Thompson go on to praise *Planned Parenthood vs. Casey.* This latest decision looks even more attractive because it clarifies problematic parts of Roe while still offering "a more positive example of the economy of moral disagreement" (87). Recall that although Casey reaffirmed women's right to terminate a pregnancy, it upheld certain restrictions on first and second trimester abortions so long as they did not impose an "undue burden" on a woman. For Gutmann and Thompson the majority opinion in Casey "illustrates one way in which pro-choice citizens can move a small but significant way toward accommodating pro-life concerns without giving up the commitment to protecting the basic liberty of women" (87). These are interesting efforts to encourage "citizens and public officials to appreciate the moral character of the positions of people with whom they disagree" (90). But how much does this really move beyond Dworkin? Gutmann and Thompson want to maintain the structure of

Roe—and praise *Roe's* appreciation for supposedly trying to preserve fetal life—without talking about transformation having to take place. Don't they simply presuppose more here than openness can allow?

Gutmann and Thompson might say that they look quite different from Dworkin (and Bohman) because, beyond the above, they suggest further efforts to support the pro-life position and these efforts do not demand transformative openness but demonstrate a willingness to support an open-mindedness that constantly renegotiates around *Roe*. For example, they talk about new public policies ensuring that pro-life advocates can refrain from contributing tax monies toward policies they deem morally unacceptable. As Gutmann and Thompson imagine it,

> all citizens should pay their fair share of taxes, but the tax monies of pro-life advocates should not contribute to subsidizing abortion, against which they have legitimate conscientious objection on deliberative grounds. . . . A better alternative for accommodation, one that reduces the complicity of pro-lifers but not their tax burden, would be voluntary contributions through the tax system to subsidize abortions—a simple check off on income tax forms, like with the three dollar contribution to the Presidential Campaign Fund that citizens now may make (89-90).

And there are additional policy options:

> Pro-choice advocates may think that publicly funded programs that help unwed mothers care for their own children are less important than pro-life proponents do, but the pro-choicers should join in actively promoting these programs and other policies that are similarly consistent with the principles they share with opponents. By trying to maximize political agreement in these ways, citizens do not end serious moral conflict, but they affirm that they accept significant parts of the substantive morality of their fellow citizens to whom they may find themselves deeply opposed in other respects (89).

The problem with this, as I see it, is that either Gutmann and Thompson truly do not believe we should sustain *Roe* and really favor instead a form of openness that allows us to sustain piecemeal agreements on abortion and the treatment of pregnancy (and perhaps only at the state level); or they really imagine, first, promoting transformation of a more dramatic sort (or simply a strong commitment to the priority of certain basic liberties) in order to sustain *Roe* and want to use this as the bedrock for further understandings, after which some general compromises can be made. Whatever the position, the point is that some confusion exists here. While Gutmann and Thompson generally want to avoid something like democratic transformative openness for fear that it will fail to acknowledge the depth of moral disagreement, they want an awful lot from their simple open-mindedness. They do call the latter a "simple virtue" (83). But if it works toward the accommodations they discuss—like the check off on the tax code and so forth—then it becomes rather difficult to see how it would allow the

Supreme Court to have made such a strong final decision about a privacy right related to abortion in the first place.

Gutmann and Thompson could say that this critique looks unfair because the kind of transformation and reconciliation that I highlighted earlier by talking about Bohman is associated with a Habermasian form of deliberative democracy and this branch of democratic theory may be subject to different problems. However, making this a key defense looks questionable. Although Gutmann and Thompson very briefly mention discourse ethics in their introduction to *Democracy and Disagreement*, their efforts to distance themselves from thinkers like Bohman or Benhabib receive almost no convincing attention. In addition, with respect to the specific issue of abortion, I would return to the point that deliberative democrats expect much from the Supreme Court and *Roe*, and note that if, overall, Gutmann and Thompson are more inclined toward very contingent agreements, they would have to live with even greater wariness toward state authority than they advocate in their recent work. If they set such a high bar for reaching mutual justifiability and appealing to "reasons that are recognizably moral in form and mutually acceptable in content" (57), and if we must do so much accommodating in middle democracy in order to get limited agreement in the wake of serious moral disagreement, there are bound to be many more frustrations or unresolved outcomes, fewer moments of convergence where the state can wield complete authoritative power. Either this is the case, and democrats like Gutmann and Thompson begin to show where they differ from others like Bohman, or both types of deliberative democracy remain subject to some similar problems and questions.

Democratic Disharmony Revisited

Gutmann and Thompson might now argue that their view of openness does not slide toward a more harmonious transformative version because they work with a cautious approach to formal legal obligations. "Neither the framework nor the claims we put forward represent final destinations or ultimate foundations. . . . The resolution of many disagreements is provisional, ever subject to new moral challenges and always open to fresh settlement" (50). Gutmann has been developing this point for some time. "This disharmony of deliberative democracy is its testimony to incommensurability and its tribute to autonomy" (Gutmann 1993b, 155). It leads often to rather "agonizing decisions" even when conversation must end (1993b, 148).

The idea is well expressed, but this does evade some difficult examples. First, for all their talk about disharmony, Gutmann and Thompson's many policy solutions show no signs of being open to challenge and serious review. Moreover, all the resolutions take place in a particular domain, presumably reinforced by state authority, and all theorizing about authority is kept at a rather limited level that sees democracy rarely in need of an ambiguous relationship to the practices of authority, including its enforcement. Others would see ambigu-

ity here as essential to a democratic project (Rosenblum 1987; Warren 199
While Gutmann and Thompson want to remain allies with these modest ske
tics, their examples tell a different story.

To buttress this point, note how frequently Gutmann and Thompson delin
ate a set of contrasting positions on an issue and then try to show how we ca
mitigate differences by developing a third option that looks to fuse elemen
from the extremes and thereby develop fully mutually respectful and moral
legitimate outcomes. On affirmative action, prayer in school, distribution
health care, the persistence of moral disagreement is considered serious, not
figment of our imagination, nor the result of simply logical inconsistencies
the part of interlocutors. However, no one has gotten the solutions to these di
agreements right. Two prominent positions contest over an issue and only whe
applying civic magnanimity do final, third solutions to abortion, affirmativ
action, organ transplants, and welfare policy emerge. Perhaps the job of the p
litical theorist requires developing an overarching set of virtues that can tal
care of our intractable problems. But if this framework aims to be more war
about complete consensus, it needs to demonstrate how reciprocity at times re
ognizes the difficulties of identifying one outcome as the morally best optic
upon which to ground (legal) authority.

Perhaps one problem lurking has to do with the way deliberative democrac
conceptualizes the relationship between legitimacy, obligation, and authorit
Modern political thought has often focused on the struggle to justify why ar
how we should obey authority given that the latter is no longer invested wi
god's will or divine right. Public principles are properly justified by consentir
or covenanting with others to recognize individuals as masters of themselve
and the source of authority with legitimate power to issue commands. Debate
have, of course, remained heated around how to consent, how much we surrer
der to or suspend judgment about authority, or how to design checks to ensu
that authority behaves as it should. Deliberative democrats emphasize how cor
sent remains most capable of legitimating when it is promoted through channe
that inform citizens about an issue and give them the power to vote or verball
approve or disapprove of a measure directly. Gutmann and Thompson recog
nize, however, that minority voices linger after democratic efforts to consolida
authority have occurred. The dissenters of any democratic system cannot b
imagined away either by clever theorizing or overzealous leadership. Demo
ratic decision-making may eventually ground decisions leading to suspension
judgment for a time as those in authority attempt to carry out "the peoples"
will. But the basis for that popular will remains open to revision since we cann
forget how gaps in agreement have the potential to unsettle public arrangement

But, again, how to insure that this caution will be realized? For Gutman
and Thompson, the best way to legitimate yet still "check" authority is throug
"accountability." Discussed in earlier articles by Gutmann, but elaborated up
at length in chapter 3 of *Democracy and Disagreement*, accountability require
that democratic representatives make public their reasons for action taken o
behalf of constituents. At least when this occurs, fewer gaps will exist betwee

those in authority and those who feel distanced from public policies their representatives support. At times representatives will even support policies that go against the majority of their direct constituents. In most cases, however, any such reasons must be subjected to public scrutiny, and representatives at every level should continue to evaluate how the reasons underlying their choices, whatever they may be, incorporate all the qualities associated with reciprocity.

Accountability is neither foolish nor implausible. Nor do deliberative democrats simply imagine a conception of authority lacking some appreciation for the disharmony resulting from moral pluralism. But the mechanism of accountability here still may not match talk of the partial consensus that deliberative democrats keep reaching for. We can explore this a bit further by noting what deliberative democrats leave out of their accountability discussion.

Deliberative democrats generally avoid mentioning two additional ways to check authority. First, they never expect those in authority should or can pull back from acting as the focal point for synthesizing disparate opinions into a coherent moral compromise and from being the guardians of higher moral truths or the bearers of our best judgment. There are times, although not necessarily inevitably and always, when those in authority should remain much more cautious about promoting either side in a debate. Authority as law remains the symbolic site for constituting who we are as citizens and holds both possibilities and dangers. A second check, closely associated with this, demands that the inherent disharmony of democracy requires any theory of authority to delineate domains where those in authority should refrain from directing commands. Such domains may not neatly divide into private and public spheres of life. Nonetheless, some such gradations of spheres could be identified and discussed in order to maintain appreciation for moral pluralism and at times attend to the ambiguity of legitimating coercive control at the margins of certain institutional arrangements. By avoiding these additional checks deliberative democrats distance themselves from the view of authority as ever capable of "neutrality" and the liberal view of authority as having to steer clear of all "private" matters where private encompasses everything in civil society that has little relation to the goal of providing physical protection. While I remain convinced that accountability is an important and desirable expectation, if deliberative democrats only promote this approach, what happens to disharmony? What happens to some of the distance needed to allow freedom to flourish? I would claim that to incorporate the additional checks noted, democrats need not forsake all efforts to incorporate accountability into a deliberative process associated with authority. But if they work with a range of checks, this could help establish the limits of transforming and harmonizing moral difference in order to expand the domain of legitimate state involvement in people's lives, and it would identify other ways to mitigate violence while acknowledging gaps in moral understanding and compatibility.

Further examples draw this out. In their own discussions of accountability, Gutmann and Thompson return to the abortion debate and try to address problems associated with individuals in authority who may make legislative choices at odds with the majority of their constituents. Take for example a representative in the U.S. Congress who supports the Supreme Court decision in *Roe* and consistently votes against certain pro-life legislative initiatives. Say the vast majority of the representative's district believes a developing fetus has constitutional "rights." How can the representative justify his or her vote? As Gutmann and Thompson see it, the representative who resists the majority's will seems to eschew reciprocity. However, if the representative gave good reasons for his or her choice in public, those could go beyond what the majority in one district deemed appropriate. Moreover, Gutmann and Thompson say that representatives can fall back on the moral weight of basic liberties to justify their support for a particular concern, like the one on abortion rights, and so long as discussion of these commitments is made public and constituents can vote a representative out of office, the situation seems reasonable. But again, we need to stop and ask an important question: where did the authority of the dominant basic liberty of *Roe* come from in the first place? As I understand it, the basis for *Roe* relates to the priority of privacy considerations and the court's determination to keep certain state-invested obligations out of the realm of decision-making related to reproduction. Without this understanding of authority and its relation to privacy as incorporated into an interpretation of *Roe*, we miss important points made by Blackmun's decision that remain capable of providing even alternative views on *Roe*. In fact, if this component of *Roe* is truly basic and highly valued, a representative need not see the authority of the decision only in relation to its synthesis of two competing moral points of view. Some "reasonable" citizens could readily argue that they are willing to support *Roe*, but generally disapprove of the court's entire range of decisions on abortion primarily because the court never went far enough to support its own, main and abiding commitment to reproductive privacy. Drucilla Cornell, who rarely talks about supporting a sweeping view of authority as forever neutral on every moral decision, nonetheless sees authority that reaches into women's reproductive decisions as deeply dangerous, capable of thwarting not only the physical but the imaginative integrity that any agent depends upon to dream of as well as move forward with life plans and meaningful goals. Where Dworkin and others have become so concerned about finding convergence in the abortion controversy, Cornell pulls back suggesting that she may be "more liberal" than Dworkin (Cornell 1995, esp. 69-89). She recognizes bodily integrity as a minimum condition of "individuation" and while individuation is not unsituated it should give us good reasons, if truly basic to our role as free and equal, to resist what looks like reciprocity in this case since not all situations necessarily need a transformation of differences if this dramatically increases control over our bodily integrity by the state. Gutmann and Thompson may be able to maintain a commitment to accountability. However, the freedom that allows for diversity may not be nurtured appropriately in every instance where authority is legitimated through reciprocal recognition. Authority granting moral pluralism space to flourish may sometimes need to take a less intrusive form.

Look at another example. Throughout the 1990s there was talk about different ways to enforce payment of child support. New initiatives to collect such funds sometimes explored ways to reach into the lives of young men especially, requiring that the latter who could not pay their designated support attend state funded job counseling and placement programs. Some programs were an attempt to break social patterns that leave young women with significant burdens to shoulder alone. Social conservatives often expressed interest in new bills expanding jobs counseling and placement programs but only if a marriage mandate could be added to existing initiatives. Statistically and morally, conservatives could have argued, marriage remains a reasonable requirement by law for a couple with a baby born out of wedlock. The state should encourage such parents to give babies the best chance in life, and the best chance is bound up with having two parents.

From a position eager to accommodate the social conservative as well as the liberal, how could a legitimate policy outcome emerge if a marriage mandate were proposed? Many would find the mandate appalling. Others would find sex out of wedlock, an abomination that, like many other social ills, deserves legal rectification. The reciprocally-sensitive solution leading to an authoritative outcome might generate a policy supporting the existing seminars for young men and add another set of classes encouraging marriage (and/or perhaps sexual abstinence outside of marriage) but no legally enforced marriage mandates. This might synthesize ideas and lead to a new, morally legitimate authoritative framework. But what about those who feel deeply disturbed about any programs promoting marriage of a certain kind by a state that claims to value privacy? Or what about those who think this policy troublesome while dealing only with men? Perhaps in an effort to satisfy critics and continue promoting legitimacy, we should not just air our differences and keep negotiating, but leave the new compromise in place and also incorporate a box on state tax forms allowing us to check off whether or not we are willing to contribute to the marriage seminars for unwed men dealing with the child support system. (Obviously this mirrors one way Gutmann and Thompson spoke of accommodating the pro-life objections to abortion.) But if we start down this path with too much vigor, problems crop up. Surely public policy making of this type can range from mildly messy to potentially obnoxious if it tries to micro-manage too many elements of moral life.

John Stuart Mill is cited at critical junctures in writing by Gutmann and Thompson and we should note how he remains a revealing companion. As a champion of liberty and autonomy he sustains significant faith in our capacity, as educated individuals, to not only use our autonomy to deliberate freely but to use discussion to reveal higher moral truths. Mill couples this with his harm principle, though it remains unclear as to how his faith in deliberation comports comfortably with his commitments to freedom. The point in voicing these concerns is not to claim that deliberative democrats are thoroughly inattentive to freedom and moral pluralism as they try to construct a conception of deliberative autonomy associated with reciprocity. We would not say this about Mill either. Deliberative democrats have much to teach about ways to struggle for legitimating authority amidst moral differences. But the requirements flowing from autonomy present important questions. Some help us solve moral conflict by replacing two sides deeply divided on an issue with a third morally secure alternative, and deliberative democrats may not consider carefully enough how their alternative can squeeze out other ways to mitigate conflict reasonably. Deliberative democrats may correctly think that more often than not we should give good reasons for a particular policy and do so with civic magnanimity. But it is not always clear why giving good reasons for an authoritative decision must actively aim to incorporate an understanding of every reciprocally magnanimous, distinct position. In some instances we may need to think about giving good reasons to let authority actively stop harm, provide conditions for choice or ensure that freedom is not eroded, but resist having authority impose too many requirements even when citizens can, in theory, imagine any number of requirements being justified by a careful synthesis of different moral perspectives.

Overall, deliberative democrats want to claim that a final, pluralism-sensitive criteria for a political theory is a chastened foundation for authority. They gesture toward promoting something between a pragmatic stalemate and a rational, discursively grounded set of rules. But such a contingent notion of legitimacy may be better imagined when we demonstrate a disciplined willingness to talk with others such that the authoritative or shared understandings that emerge remain clearly open to renegotiation. Moreover, such tentative bridges across boundaries may be drawn between adversaries who approach each other as capable of what we can call agency rather than autonomy. In the chapters to follow, I ask whether a notion of agency (leading to what I will identify as equal regard vs. mutual respect) not only proves more open to diverse groups and cautious toward transformation but also fulfills other democratic goals. I expect that an equality ethic built on my view will not require abandoning democracy. Rather I will consider this alternative appropriate for sustaining effective aspects of democratic inclusion while carefully preserving the "disharmony" that deliberative democrats prize.

Chapter 4

Strong Pluralism
and Moral Incommensurability

My earlier critiques were prompted by a paradox. Our equal standing based on a set of shared capacities or needs introduces certain duties and fair limits on public interactions. However, once introduced, such expectations create boundaries and exclusions. We imagine those as desirable or at least "reasonable." But this does not always follow. Is there any way to secure a general notion of fairness based on what we imagine makes us equals while trying to ensure that diversity is acknowledged and placed in high regard?

Stanley Fish, for one, rejects this question. He claims the (many and often unexpected) exclusions resulting from a priori assumptions about equality mean so-called fair principles, civil rules and boundaries will *always* be illegitimate. Finding an ideal "balance" between equality and diversity is an illusion. I examine Fish's skepticism about equality assumptions briefly in this chapter and argue for avoiding his "realist" reaction to the problem I have tried to address. Fish's work demands we drop a common vision of equality and let citizens face each other as distinct opponents ready to do (only verbal?) battle ("weapon in hand" (Fish 1999, 14)) due to their incommensurable points of view. Better to recognize, Fish writes, that "political liberalism . . . can be a resource for politics, not for politics in the rarefied sense named by chimeras like fairness and mutual respect but for politics as it has always been practiced, and practiced honorably in the wards and boroughs of ancient Rome, seventeenth-century London, and twentieth-century Chicago" (13).

Before confronting Fish, I lay some groundwork for supporting alternative expectations for equality. I agree that many prominent views may disappoint or fail to acknowledge their own inconsistencies. I also agree, as Fish notes, that part of the difficulty here relates to an unwillingness to see the depth of what many call strongly incommensurable moral outlooks. But if incommensurability exists, it does not necessarily result in *severe* incomprehensibility where mitigating differences (legitimately) requires giving up on *any* morally acceptable common ground and letting the strongest (or the simple local majority?) win the day, as Fish seems to claim. Incommensurability may exist in degrees; and even if strong, its condition may require some mutual intelligibility to be understood even as a condition of conflict. Moreover, we can and should continue to imagine points for comparability, with the hope that our suggestions might do better than others.

The thinkers reviewed earlier believe something similar, so I will not part company completely with them. By comparison, however, I discuss how assumptions about what I will call the capacity for agency may be attractive and more acceptable to a diverse citizenry than assumptions about our capacity for autonomy. I claim my expectations can and should be placed on the register of options available. Exactly how my alternative connects and contrasts with others receives more attention in chapters 5 and 6. This chapter stays focused on: 1. characterizing what we might mean when referring to moral pluralism and moral incommensurability, and how incommensurability may exist in degrees not only in a severe form; 2. how agency may be a point for comparability when certain levels of incommensurability exist but nonviolent coexistence is desired; 3. why I do not wish to agree wholeheartedly with Fish who believes incommensurability exists primarily in the extreme; and how I also reject a position like James Griffin's which (contra Fish) tells us not to worry about moral incommensurability at all.

Strong Moral Pluralism and Moral Incommensurability

Having suggested that certain thinkers may not leave enough room for moral pluralism and strong conflicts in the course of characterizing equality, let me define more carefully what I mean by moral pluralism, how it is linked to moral incommensurability, and how the latter often exists in degrees.

"Moral pluralism" is a phrase most frequently used to describe a condition of diversity that, as Amelie Rorty puts it (1990, 11), "validates and endorses distinctive and competing ideals and principles, virtues and values." "Social societies—particularly those with a strong and homogeneous religious orientation—have a high degree of consensus on the direction and measure of basic norms and values. But most contemporary western European societies are hospitable to pluralism of principle: the basic values that implicitly guide the conduct and aspirations of their members vary considerably, not always along cultural or religious lines" (11).[1] Joseph Raz defines moral pluralism much as Rorty does

(Raz 1986, 395), but ultimately associates this general definition with a "weak" kind of pluralism.

> Moral pluralism claims not merely that incompatible forms of life are morally acceptable but that they display distinct virtues, each capable of being pursued for its own sake. . . . Two lives must differ in the virtues they display or in the degree that they display them, if they are to count as belonging to different forms of life. A form of life is maximal if, under normal circumstances, a person whose life is of that kind cannot improve it by acquiring additional virtues, nor by enhancing the degree to which he possesses any virtue, without sacrificing another virtue he possesses or the degree to which it is present in his life. Belief in value pluralism is the belief that there are several maximal forms of life (396).

Raz adds that "strong" moral pluralism requires the "addition of one or more of the following three claims" each of which depend upon the existence of some form of moral incommensurability:

> First, the incompatible virtues are not completely ranked relative to each person (who is part of a way of life or social form). That is, it is not the case that for each person all the incompatible virtues can be strictly ordered according to their moral worth, so that he ought to pursue the one which for him has the highest worth, and his failure to do so disfigures him with a moral blemish, regardless of his success in pursuing other, incompatible, moral virtues. Second, the incompatible virtues are not completely ranked by some impersonal criteria of moral worth. Even if the first condition obtains it is still possible to claim that, though there is no moral blemish on me if I am a soldier and excel in courage because I am made of bronze, excellence in dialectics, which is incompatible with courage and is open only to those made of gold, is a superior excellence by some moral standards which are not relative to the character or conditions of life of individuals. . . . Third, the incompatible virtues exemplify diverse fundamental concerns. They do not derive from a common source, or from common ultimate principles (396-97).

Bernard Williams clarifies these links as well, noting that "there are at least four different denials which the claim (of incommensurability) can be taken to involve" (1981, 77). In listing them, Williams suggests levels of "increasing strength, so that accepting one later in the list involves accepting those earlier." (I alter Williams's language slightly here, though the list is essentially his.)

1. There is no one common currency—the most notable and likely being utility which reduces all other values to a single mental state—in terms of which values can be ranked and conflicts between them resolved.

2. There is no "independent value" or procedure—which I take to be something like an objective hierarchy of values (Platonic) or a transcendental procedure such as Kantian universalizing—that can be appealed to in order to compare, rank or resolve each conflict of values.

3. There is no value (independent or not) that can be appealed to in order to

compare, rank and resolve each conflict of value.

4. No conflict of values can ever rationally be resolved.

Moral pluralism marked by *severe* situations of moral incommensurability might occur when all four of the "denials" above exist. In such situations we might lack critical overlapping reference points through which to understand or even hope to identify others as "equals" or cooperative companions. Perhaps this is imaginable in the most fanciful of cases, in meetings between seemingly sentient beings from different planets. Some would consider confrontation or encounters between different cultures, one past the other present, also generating this kind of severe breakdown in understanding. Bernard Williams discusses these as "notional" confrontations (Williams 1985, 160).

Moral pluralism might also involve conflicts shaped by *strong* incommensurability. The latter could be identified with the first three denials, sometimes with the fourth. But this should look less extreme, requiring at least a fuller set of background conditions in order to make sense of the conflict at hand. We might consider situations where tragic cases or dilemmas exist. The famous Antigone faces two duties—performing a family burial or obeying laws decreed by the ruler of the polis. The tragedy lacks intensity (or the mark of strong incommensurability) unless understood against the context of ancient Greek women's obligations to the home and the importance of leadership to the polis. The reference to context at least blunts total unintelligibility. Other disagreements between Antigone and Creon might be resolved through reference to some additional shared understanding. But the conflict Antigone faces demonstrates strong incommensurability—in this particular case, if one chooses to fulfill one valued duty, the other is not annulled, just simultaneously refused. Moreover, considerable loss is felt by the individual who chooses to act on either duty and reasons for the loss are at least understood.

Other types of comparisons demonstrate similar points. Take those between friendship and money making. As Joseph Raz notes, many (in our society) consider such values incommensurable (1986, ch. VIII, esp. 336-37). We cannot compare friendship or other relationships (such as those with a significant other, spouse, parent, sibling) to an impersonal exchange or make friendship into a means rather than an end in itself. Incomparability does not result from the "nature of" the objects under review. The capacity to be a friend or spouse in a society like our own often requires "psychological attributes" such as "interest in other people, empathy with them" and so on (350). Simultaneously, this example still requires an ability to understand how certain conventional practices give offense, express affection, or show respect. One needs the capacity to understand how these actions, like the willingness to exchange time or relations with one's spouse for money, can undermine one's relationship (349).

What makes many values incomparable, as Raz puts it, is the "symbolic significance" of the values in different circumstances. Raz qualifies this point by acknowledging that "symbolic significance" may be "in the eye of the beholder." Someone may not see certain actions as meaningful. However, this does not mean that [an individual]can disregard symbolic reasons with impunity. Two situations have to be distinguished. A person may believe that holding there to be a price for companionship is incompatible with having loving relations with one's spouse and still he may come to view his relations with his spouse as having a price. He is then disloyal, and he damages his relations with his spouse, perhaps irretrievably so. On the other hand he may not believe that it has that significance. He may believe that everything has its price. . . . In such a case he never had the relations with his spouse of which belief in incommensurability is a symbolic constituent (351).

The individual in this example is not "irrational" (353). He is disqualified from a certain kind of relationship, and this may be consciously chosen. The main point is that in some cases, talk of incommensurability can only occur if much else is understood, if other conventions are seen as "constitutive" of the values under review (352).[2]

What about *weaker* incommensurability? Note that Williams' list does not dismiss common ways to rank or resolve conflicts in some cases. Incommensurability denies that one scale, value, principle, view of well-being can rank or settle each and every set of differences. Weaker incommensurability may exist where we have distinctiveness with tentative prioritizing.

For example, consider the difference between a commitment to freedom versus equality. Equality (of material well-being, say) may enhance free speech, but it is not necessarily the same as (nor many would say inherently better or worse than) the exercise of free speech. However, the incomparability between these two values can face compromises. In specific cases, we do try to show how promoting material well-being may enhance certain liberties and hence should take precedence under certain conditions; or how coercion has strangled freedom of movement so severely for so many that concerns about providing a more egalitarian mode of food distribution, for example, may become a secondary concern. Recognition that trade-offs between such values will occur need not eliminate the distinctiveness of each. Moreover, with each trade-off we may face regrets, leaving concerns unresolved but worthy of future attention. Unlike tragic cases or dilemmas (where the options for actions lead to a wrongdoing of some kind), the conditions here look less problematic. Liberty, even if prized, is not expected to "trump" always. And the loss a person may feel when liberty is diminished for the sake of a procedure sustaining equality or fairness, say, is not likely to generate anguish (at least not as notably in our society) on the order of magnitude encountered by Antigone. Weak incommensurability may account for strong differences between certain values but characterize clashes less troublesome to resolve.

Bridging Boundaries

Some will consider this discussion incomplete. Notably, moral incommensurability sounds like an endorsement for relativism (which sees others—their perspectives, values, beliefs, styles of life—acceptable in their own place). And this position is often rejected as incoherent.

Incommensurability does undermine objectivism when it suggests that two outlooks or ways of life "exclude one another," but this need not (instantly) lead to each side abandoning judgment and actually accepting another's position as equally good. As Bernard Williams puts it: "Someone who has certain dispositions and expectations as a member of one culture will often be unwilling, when confronted with an alternative way of life, to do what is done in the other culture. Moreover, it is part of what makes his responses ethical responses that they are deeply internalized enough for his reaction, in some cases, to be not merely unwillingness but rejection" (Williams 1985, 158). Any moral position by definition will likely "stretch beyond its boundaries" (159). Take the potentially intense clash between a modern industrial and "hypertraditional" society. As Williams observes, when the traditional society "is first exposed to another culture and invited to reflect, it cannot suddenly discover that there is an implicit relativization hidden in its language. It will always be, so to speak, too early or too late for that. It is too early, when they have never reflected or thought of an alternative to 'us.'. . . It is too late, when they confront the new situation; that requires them to see beyond their existing rules and practices" (158-59). Incommensurability, if and when it exists, does not mean that we retain highly contingent or loose connections to our perspectives; or that we cannot feel intensely disturbed by the reasons others give for their claims.

Assuming, then, that moral pluralism is linked to incommensurability, various tactics, modes of self discipline, or common understandings should be envisioned to deal with the loss of a single "ahistorical matrix or framework" through which "we can ultimately appeal in determining the nature of rationality, acknowledge, truth, reality, goodness or rightness" on all occasions (Bernstein 1983, 8). Assuming we want to quell certain forms of violence and often mitigate the intensity of incommensurability, what expectations can accomplish this?

In instances of *severe* incommensurability, we might acknowledge the existence of others even if they are deeply distant and self contained, even if we are disdainful of them and common ground is limited in the extreme. To avoid violence, we may be able to acknowledge shared desires for self preservation and stop short of imposing our views due to fear. This may lead to low level frustration, even weary indifference toward the other. There may be stalemates and grudging acknowledgments, sometimes toleration, and not likely anything like consensus, convergence, and or collaborations. *Strong* moral incommensurability may present further options. Certain kinds of tragic situations demonstrate deep distance between individuals. But even here background conditions exist in order to understand when and how such painful dilemmas can occur. Working with these limited understandings, we may step back from the most intense differences to suspend judgment to let others be while holding on to a series of formal guidelines that help mitigate violence. The situation may still ask us to extend ourselves to others, to acknowledge that they are purposive and deserve to be regarded with civility as imaginative, thinking, planning beings like ourselves. This may look more generous than putting up with one another even as we ask others to hold off trying to convert different individuals to another point of view. In the end, this may allow for coexistence that looks less precarious than a stalemate and more tempered than toleration. Going beyond this, we could acknowledge our shared capacities for imaginative planning and rule following; commit to listen and exchange with others to remain civil and responsive to re-evaluating how well common institutions provide opportunities for others to follow their life plans. This may, in turn, lead to tentative collaborations and to stretching across boundaries and to more than simply coexistence.

The point is that all of these are possibilities; they acknowledge that different levels of incommensurability may come with different ways to bridge differences. A common conception of freedom and substantive elements associated with an ethic of equality can be part of a continuum, one related to the intensity of our gaps in understanding. A capacity for autonomy and its attendant virtues, like reciprocity, should make room for other options. (Strong moral incommensurability, for example, might require starting from assumptions about a common vision of agency and civility. Autonomy and respect might be more feasible when weaker forms of moral incommensurability exist.) A more developed view of agency with an ethic of civility remains for chapters 5 and 6. But these comments set up a segue into those chapters and start to suggest how appreciation for strong moral incommensurability prompts alternatives.

However, before moving ahead, I want to address two critics, Stanley Fish and James Griffin. They would consider the entire discussion thus far unnecessary or misguided. Fish would reject efforts to acknowledge strong moral incommensurability and then tame it with a priori assumptions about agency, or any other abstract, generalized vision of what "we" share as humans or citizens. A politics committed to sustaining broad participation never achieves legitimacy under such circumstances. The only way to embrace differences fully (and fairly) is with pragmatic, "ad hoc" political solutions. James Griffin would attack my comments from another angle. He finds anxiety about strong incommensurability altogether foolish. Ways of life may diverge but rarely look incomparable or tragically incompatible. Fish and Griffin are addressed below. To my mind, each misses nuanced dilemmas by seeing incommensurability as severe or nonexistent; neither should undercut the direction subsequent chapters pursue.

The Trouble with Incommensurability

Facing Fish's Skepticism

Stanley Fish has relentlessly chastised almost every liberal or democratic theorist of note, especially thinkers like Rawls and Gutmann.[3] He sees most of-fering disingenuous efforts to describe and accommodate "fundamental" moral or cultural differences. First, such efforts misunderstand moral incommensura-bility. If you take fundamental disagreement seriously, as so many claim to, you will rarely establish common ground prior to letting opposing positions meet, explore their differences, and clash. Fish expresses this as a kind of social fact about moral incommensurability. Take the secularist and deeply religious indi-vidual. The latter might suggest that sexual preferences cannot be used to judge fitness in the workplace: all individuals deserve the equal opportunity to pursue their life plans and desires; certain activities are private and none of the public's business; a religiously based condemnation of behavior cannot be used to justify a public policy in a multicultural society, and so forth. The religious individual simply will not agree to these assumptions and cannot be asked to put the secu-larist's understanding of the self first, draining all contents from the core of moral personality. The "truly" religious individual sees homosexual desire as deeply sinful, never something to respect or treat with civility. Or think of the abortion debate. As Fish puts it: "If abortion is murder, why does one have an obligation to be fair to would be murderers by legalizing their crime?" (1999, 209). He continues:

> A pro-life advocate sees abortion as a sin against a god who infuses life at the moment of conception; a pro-choice advocate sees abortion as a decision to be made in accordance with the best scientific opinion as to when the beginning of life, as we know it, occurs. No conversation between them can ever get started because each of them starts from a different place, and they could never agree as to what they were conversing about. . . . The 'content of a belief' is a func-tion of its source, and the critique of one will always be the critique of the other. Of course we can say and do say, 'I don't care where you got that idea from; it's wrong.' But what we mean is that we can't see where such an idea came from, and we can't see that because the place it came from is not one where we have ever been; it is the place, the source, we object to even when we fail—we could hardly succeed and be ourselves—to recognize it (256).

No political or moral theory can really appreciate or recognize the depth of diversity if it fails to see the severity of incommensurability. As a result, no po-sition should expect to "remake" itself (Fish 1999, 256-57) before political ar-gument gets underway.

Thinkers like the ones reviewed earlier nevertheless present their assump-tions as "natural," "rational," or so thin as to be relatively "neutral." Whether free speech liberals (who believe they support a neutral principle best for all

(1999, ch. 5-7) or more virtue oriented theorists, like Gutmann and Thompson (ch. 4, 9), these positions face similar problems. Gutmann and Thompson, for example, criticize racial discrimination, but the whole effort is partial and intolerant, as Fish sees it. He writes the following characterization of Gutmann and Thompson's ideas:

> Anyone who favors racial discrimination is just sick [Gutmann and Thompson imply] and has no reason except hate and prejudice; if he has reasons, they are unaccompanied by evidence; if he has evidence, it is the wrong kind; if he has the right kind, it is not as good as the evidence we have. You know that they could go on forever in this vein because all they [Gutmann and Thompson] are doing is negotiating a very small circle that begins and ends with their own prior conviction and a vocabulary made in its image. . . . To be sure, there are repeated attempts to present this in-house parochialism as if it were the expression of an impersonal and general rule, as when they described their position as issuing from 'a disinterested perspective that could be adopted by any member of society' and distinguish it from the 'implausible beliefs' of those who cite the Bible or law of nature. But aren't those for whom the Bible's authoritative also members of society, and isn't the fact that these believers-citizens refuse the authors' perspective evidence that it is not disinterested at all? And isn't 'disinterest' one more word—like impartial and reasonable—that claims the high ground of neutrality while performing exclusionary work? (195-96).

Elsewhere, Fish punctuates the point with rhetorical questions: "Who gets to say what is or is not a plausible premise? And how is that premise plausible (a real weasel word) to millions of people who have been ruled out of court in advance? The answers are obvious and embarrassing because they all point to an act of power, a peremptory exclusion and dismissal, that cannot be acknowledged as such lest the liberal program of renouncing power and exclusion be exposed for the fiction it surely is" (201). Fish also blames liberalism past for this approach to politics. John Locke's letter on toleration with its dismissive views on religion in public life has clearly shaped modern expectations on these matters (ch. 9).

Such concerns are complemented by a final point. As Fish puts it, a truly pluralism sensitive politics must be politics "all the way down," meaning, as I understand it, that a politics attentive to diversity must be conducted "ad hoc," divorced from everyone else's morality other than what Fish calls the "morality of taking sides, of frank and vigorous political action, that is celebrated (not urged; it is inevitable) in the pages (of [Fish's] book)" (14). The allies for such an "inevitable" project include Hobbes, Dewey, Rorty, and Machiavelli. *The Prince* deserves particular praise for its realism and emphasis on disdain for a politics governed by general moral rules or formal universal guidelines. Given the incoherence and illegitimacy of others' ideals, we should side only with those, like Machiavelli, who understand the need for a political culture where friends side against enemies and where (to repeat) "political liberalism . . . can be a resource for politics, not for politics in the rarefied sense named by chimeras like fairness and mutual respect but for politics as it has always been practiced, and practiced honorably in the wards and boroughs of ancient Rome, seventeenth-century London, and twentieth-century Chicago" (13).

I, too, voiced reservations about the "reasonableness" and hidden exclusions of certain assumptions about equality. So why not agree with Fish's bold conclusions?

Fish's expectations, especially about moral incommensurability, remain extreme—unnuanced and too focused on severe cases of incompatibility. And his underdeveloped expectations for politics remain naïve, as I see them. Fish fails to value the paradoxical struggle that often must exist for holding onto broad levels of participation, while also establishing reasonable limits on public action. Politics is about constant re-negotiations over such issues, not simply about finding ways to completely dismiss all such efforts. Tension between the particular and the universal that often preoccupy political theorists as well as practitioners is not overcome by resorting to simple ad hoc decision making as the (new universal) norm. In addition, if I read Fish correctly, he is not only criticizing taken-for-granted generalizations as dangerous, but valorizing a local or neighborhood politics of the people without making any discrimination between politics guided by local party bosses whom one might admire and those needing serious checks from higher level, general rules.

To explain further, let me return to moral incommensurability. This chapter has explored the intelligibility of thinking about incommensurability in degrees. Severe incommensurability can sound quite extreme. If Fish expects us to confront that condition, he may correctly conclude that little can be done to resolve a situation without violence. But if what he describes is more like strong incommensurability, he forgets that this may be predicated on the existence of overlapping background conditions. Raz reinforced this point noting how the very intelligibility of intractable differences or tragic conflicts assumes some common understandings. Of course, Fish could still say that no such conditions will provide *principled understanding* in advance for resolving serious conflict. Again, imagine a religious individual and a committed secularist; they could share much if they lived in the United States, but if they came from different regions of the country and remained divided in their spiritual outlooks, it is hard to deny that their experiences would filter through highly distinctive lenses. But the question for Fish is, why create such a rigid secular/religious dichotomy? Do individuals characterize themselves like this in most instances? Why never assess places for overlap? Perhaps because this suits Fish's argument. Fish rarely examines situations other than those where religious and secular matters clash in the extreme and among individuals who seem to embody the ends of what must be a spectrum of differences depending upon the situation or issue at hand. Moreover, Fish accuses many religious writers, interested in finding common ground alongside liberal secular principles, of being unable to understand the true basic starting premises of a faith-based mind set. These wayward Christians are often university or divinity school based writers, apparently unwittingly drawn into a liberal, academic mindset, and they are dismissed. Their ideas cannot be part of any imagined spiritual life (see esp. ch. 12 and 10). But again, there is no continuum. Fish never even shows much empirical support for how his view of a properly religious mindset is the reality most embody. There is not even an effort made to examine carefully other writers from different religious traditions (often "fundamental" or orthodox) where efforts to work with liberal or universal principles of human rights, and the like, are pursued (Bauer and Bell 1999; Van Ness 1999; Peters and Wolper 1995; Bloom, Martin, and Proudfoot 1996). Are they too missing the basic idea of what it means to be religious?

I would also add that many of our most serious clashes pitting religion and secular perspectives revolve around reproduction and control not only over women's bodies but other's bodies seen as property and incapable of will or reasoned action. Claiming that these views come from radically different moral outlooks or religious versus secular understandings may be too simplistic a starting point.[4] While a religious practice does involve bending one's will to that of a higher being and/or spiritual community, I find nothing simply "western" about suggesting that practices adhered to because of threat of physical harm (chastity for many women enforced by social and economic ostracization and/or fear of "honor" killing) are not necessarily about maintaining spirituality. A will broken is not necessarily a will bent toward god. Is it only "secular" to say that humans when acting *even within religious practices* need to be acknowledged as actors with choice, not automatons? Doesn't religious scripture itself emphasize the need for individual acceptance of a spiritual way of life, otherwise hypocrisy results? Isn't something like agency (marked by an ability to carry out purposive action) "necessary" as part of the "human condition" even when someone is acting in a religious capacity? Is it secular and western to say there is a distinction between practices adhered to by inculcation complemented by choice and those adhered to through oppression and violence?

Perhaps these questions are undercut by the possibility, as Fish could remind us, that many religious traditions see women first as reproductive entities and men's property, and not fully capable of exercising agency at all. Perhaps this "different" claim is worth hearing and getting out into public view. But why not say it remains highly contestable given what we now discern about women's capacity to act as purposive actors? Fish may be missing something about the examples he cites and what it means to exhibit severe moral incommensurability. Simultaneously he may be far too skeptical about whether very minimal expectations can be used to justify a position's (moral) standing and to reject physical threats to a body looking to act within a shared practice.

Finally there is Fish on politics. On the one hand, Fish clearly projects himself as a good democrat, a man of the people who believes moral opponents deserve opportunities to be "defeated in combat" (68). He never wants a moral position declared "ineligible before the fight begins" (68), and he wants to expose the lack of generosity voiced by the academic elite (with their misguided use of rationality as "an engine of exclusion and boundary making" (70)). But while boundary making and laws may be messy, imperfect, and open to reevaluation, are we to engage in combat each and every time we hit differences over public policy? Aren't there ways in which the "fight" is not appropriate, especially when certain levels of violence are involved? Where are the distinctions here?

Again, turn to abortion. Under the reading Fish gives of an antiabortion point of view, resistance and possibly violence could sound justified. Would Fish set no general limits here? If he supports limits, are they imposed for the sake of state order only; do arguments never sound legitimate when offered in the name of "our constitution" or based on general respect for the choice of women or the need to find a balanced set of understandings about control over the reproductive process? Fish suggests that politics at many (or all?) points is ultimately about imposition and we might as well accept it. Is politics never about groping for boundaries and limits that avoid violence for good reasons, reasons that could be reevaluated even as they get constructed as the ungrounded but now existing "bedrock" of certain shared understandings?

In addition, should we assume that Fish's approval of Hobbes and Machiavelli includes support for their views on the state? Recall Hobbes on the chaos which starts from the danger of moral words and individual desires (1986, I, ch. 5; 6) Although Fish may reject Hobbes' atomized theory of language learning and individual development, he appears to imagine a similar atomized condition for groups. If so, why not follow *Leviathan* and *The Prince* to their conclusions? For both, the state or a political leader must master the unpredictability brought by "fortune" or moral language, possibly use religion for state ends, and exercise considerable control over public life.

But let's assume that Fish does not want to accept this either. Rather his moral skepticism supports a more local effort to muddle along, establish laws, and settle some disputes for a time (1999, ch. 4). We reject talk of general rights or protections, perhaps, but what generalizations can be drawn upon to hold a larger society together? And how might we thwart a bureaucrat like a Robert Moses or local democratic structures that too often hold their own dangers and limits?

Fish might claim that I am saddling him with too much baggage. In a gesture, frequently used at the end of several chapters, Fish wants to insist that he criticizes others but that he cannot offer solutions once exposing dangers. (1996, 113, 150) This strategy of avoidance about "the good" is inadequate (does he speak from a morally neutral "nowhere"?), and seems undermined by the references regarding Machiavelli and Hobbes. But of course, if Fish is serious, if he does not have any alternative in mind after offering his critiques, perhaps the direction I hope to pursue will not look so troublesome after all. Indeed, the upshot of Fish's critique could be different: why not, after showing troubles with principles, demonstrate the need to be more cautious when creating them, tentative when suggesting that they are well grounded in absolute universal assumptions, and mindful of the exclusions that certain equality assumptions establish, checking those exclusions and altering situations as needed? Why not say tensions exist in public life that never neatly resolve, and why not continue to reach for commonalities and generalizations about equality that we need but may wish to imagine with greater sensitivity instead of abandoning them altogether?

Doubting Incommensurability

In his book *Well-being*, James Griffin (1986) discusses a continuum of ways to describe moral incommensurability. Strong incommensurability receives attention and its plausibility is rejected. We need to now look closely at Griffin since his suggestions could make all the anxieties I have introduced seem seriously overblown.

Overall, Griffin agrees with the obvious description of moral incommensurability. (The condition exists if, given two values A and B, A is "neither more valuable than B, nor less, and not of equal value" (1986, 79).) However, he pursues five examples in an effort to dismiss it as completely unlikely.

Griffin turns first to tragic cases. Admittedly we often face "painful" choices. Some (identified as tragic) make us believe strong value clashes can exist: "A talented but chronically depressed person may have to choose between suicide and accomplishment. And the two values, freedom from pain and accomplishment, are so far removed from one another that they are scarcely easy to compare" (80). But these kinds of struggles should not lead to conceptual confusion. "True incomparability arises not when we cannot decide how to rank values but when we decide that they are unrankable. And this is not a case in which, since life forces choices upon us, we choose but do not prefer" (80). Griffin wants to emphasize two points: that indecision is one thing and incommensurability another—the latter need not result from the former; and that more often than not we do choose between two seemingly different values, demonstrating that some ranking or weighing takes place and can be articulated. If we dwell on the above example for a moment, we can see that one often weighs each value against the other. "If the pain is great enough and the accomplishment slight enough, we should not consider the accomplishment worth the pain" (80). We don't simply throw ourselves thoughtlessly toward one option.

These two points—(i) that serious indecision does not indicate incommensurability and that more often we are faced with the former rather than the latter, and (ii) that weighing or ranking generally goes on in order for us to judge between options and make a choice—are reinforced through another: that what we call incommensurability is often best categorized as something altogether different, (iii) perhaps rough equality or, as Griffin later discusses, non-equivalence or irreplaceability.

Imagine two artists, novelists A and B, demonstrating "very diverse achievements." Griffin describes A as "dry but full of insight, B unperceptive but hilarious" (80). While we "often despair" in trying to rank different virtues or talents, the fact is that we often do find gradations in these artists' abilities—and then sort out different reasons to value one over the other. We assess the significance of A's insights or B's humor, and then "strictly speaking" we rank the value of insight and amusement as "values to us" (80). Moreover, when ranking proves challenging, we usually call such values roughly the same, not simply incomparable. The "roughness is not in our understanding but ineradicably in the values themselves." Often we cannot say that, in every instance, insight is going to prove more important than being amused. But we can give some general sense of their importance in relation to each other for most of us most of the time. Rough equality promotes "vague" rather than "strong" orderings (81).

Charles Taylor, along with others, cites yet a third type of incommensurability. This does not, however, look like indecision or rough equality. Some values or things are above exchange, Taylor notes. They are "incommensurably higher." For example, a person such as Mother Teresa would consider a Christian notion of agape incomparable to other values; others might consider personal integrity or commitments to national heritage or to religious fundamentalism life's most worthy commitments. Most of us acquire over a lifetime special goals "bound up with our sense of the qualitative contrasts in our lives" (Taylor 1985 ii., 240). These "stand out above others" (1985, 236) and cannot be ranked without being debased. Incommensurability of this sort must remain plausible if we hope to have a meaningful life.

Griffin grants plausibility to Taylor's examples. They remind us, in some ways, similar to Raz's situations with "constitutive" incommensurability. But Griffin determines, as above, that thinkers generally confuse incommensurability with an altogether different type of relationship. True, many things "constitute what we think of as the dignity of human existence, central among them being autonomy and liberty." And "if we surrender our human standing, we shall find no equivalent" (1986, 81). Griffin cites Martha Nussbaum as another contemporary moralist who highlights, rightly so, the notion of irreplaceable values. However, these types of examples turn out again to equate incomparability with ideas that do not necessarily imply an inability to rank.

For Griffin, Taylor, and others like Nussbaum discuss non-equivalence or even irreplaceability. But this need not eliminate comparisons. We might say that nothing equals or "can take the place of human standing." But this "is not to say that nothing can even be ranked with it as to value. In fact, in rare cases, other values can even outrank it. If for some unfortunate person autonomy brings extreme anxiety, it might be better to sacrifice some autonomy" (82). We make trade-offs, even of human lives, all the time. "The French government knows that each year several drivers lose their lives because of the beautiful roadside avenues of trees, yet they do not cut them down. Even aesthetic pleasure is (rightly) allowed to outrank a certain number of human lives. . . . We want to express our sense of the enormous value of certain things—human standing, an individual human life—and once again we reach for strong expressions" (82). Non-equivalence is not necessarily incomparability.

Perhaps some will say, with Nussbaum, that what we are really discussing is "irreplaceability." This is a stronger term and perhaps more likely to prompt incomparability, Griffin acknowledges. But still, Griffin claims this will not change his ideas. A person may be called irreplaceable. But, for example, "when a child dies, the parents might have another child whom they would not otherwise have had. Or when his wife dies, a man might remarry. And these new relationships can enrich one's life as much as the old. It does not destroy grief that one can love again, or that the new love be as valuable as the old. . . . The irreplaceability of individuals is not the incommensurability of values" (82, n. 18). A particular person or thing might be irreplaceable, but the general value that caring for that person or thing expresses can take a new form. The existence of new forms of the same value is what allows us to continue to make comparisons properly.

Finally, beyond these examples, some cite incommensurable clashes between "world views" or "radically different metaphysics." Griffin thinks this has limits too. Such radical differences are "doubtful," he writes. "We are interested in whether some of the values we use are incomparable, and if two sets of values are themselves incomparable as to plausibility and we must just opt between them, then, though the sets are incomparable, we use only one. And if we do in fact wish to use both sets of values, as doubtless sometimes we do, then we shall be forced to organize them." Again, the need to choose and our capacity for reflectiveness must involve ranking.

> For instance, self-denial, contemplation, and solitude come out of a religious world view, and they are not in the ordinary sense prudential values. They may be matters of vocation, and a calling from God. . . . World views may clash in a way that allows us to choose only one. Or they may clash in a way that allows us to choose both, but then they ought themselves to show something about the relative status of the values they propose. They should show us how to rank all of them. Some values may indeed outrank others. But this is not incomparability any longer, but some weaker form of incommensurability (82-83).

Tragic cases, clashes between "irreplaceable" values, clashes between world views—these all prompt use of the term incommensurability. Griffin sees mental rubbish cluttering such usage. However, in the process of clarification, Griffin may have pushed away important questions and experiences. (Don't values such as friendship lose their meaning when compared to some things like money; don't we find ourselves wanting often to say that some things are incomparably "higher" than others? Aren't some artists working in different mediums incomparable? Are we always able to compare world views past and future with the present?)

Joseph Raz takes these points further and I turn to his reflections in closing to contrast his ideas with Griffin's. Again, my goal is not to deny that incommensurability may be one among many ways to describe differences. But incommensurability does have a place among a continuum of ways to talk about moral conflict.

Raz's Response

Recall Griffin's earlier points about tragedies or dilemmas. They may be rare, as Griffin suggests. But are agents who face two significantly wrong (not simply unpalatable) options just wavering, indecisive characters? Ideally, as

agents we choose, act, judge, and finalize decisions. Generally, we do not simply rest in limbo to ponder or whine about the difficulties of a choice indefi-
nitely or without reasons for action. Griffin never wants us to ignore this.
Nonetheless, in trying to remove serious obstacles to decision-making, Griffin
has to argue that when we choose, dilemmas evaporate.

But dilemmas, and the different identity perspectives that often generate
them, are neither dismissible, reduced to the mental state of indecisiveness, nor
likely to dissolve even when choices force themselves on us. How dilemmas
occur is not something to tackle in detail here. What can be asserted is that these
kinds of cases rarely sound so implausible as to be dismissed, that even Griffin's
own example can be turned into a more serious dilemma than he allows, and that
the language of incommensurability may highlight the difficulty of choosing
between wrongdoings likely to emerge from a dilemma.

Raz describes "two classes" of moral dilemmas:

> Some are said to be cases in which one of the agent's options is clearly the
> better one, or at least involves the lesser evil. In such cases there is a right
> course of action. One would be in the wrong if one failed to take the right ac-
> tion. Nevertheless, it is claimed, performing the right action does not mean that
> one does not do a wrong. Harming another or failing one's duty in the imagined
> circumstances is a wrong even if it is, on balance, the best and the only right
> thing to do. The second type of case is different. In it there is no right or best
> action. All the avenues which are open to one are wrong. Whatever one does
> one would be doing evil or wronging another (1986, 359).

In both situations described, the only options available would lead to harm or
wrongful acts. These differ from a host of other situations where we face unpalatable options; or where we might be able to take actions that are wrong in some
circumstances but right in others. The difficulty faced by an individual who "has
to choose between traveling by air, of which he is terrified and which he finds
unpleasant, and losing an attractive job" (361) is not the same as a situation
where any option leads to wrongdoing. But even if the latter scenarios are more
likely, this does not give good grounds for dismissing the "conceptual room" for
dilemmas. And if one wants to make a distinction between the case of the fright-
ened airplane passenger's choice and Antigone's choice, a discussion of dilemmas is helpful.

Moreover, when an individual is found "tortured" by a dilemma, it need not
be the product of indecisiveness or weakness of will. We would rarely say that
many situations held up as dilemmas are really painful because the individuals
who face the choices lacks character. The character of the choice seems to present the more notable problem. Certainly Griffin's own example could be more
sensitively conceived if we imagine his troubled individual (in the prime of life
with a number of duties and obligations to others that will be significantly af-
fected by the individual's suicide or his ongoing actions colored by deep depres-
sion) possibly facing a variation on a dilemma rather than displaying an indeci-

sive nature. Griffin has given us little reason to suspect that only indecision is at play. Indeed, many would also say that to acknowledge this offers some important alternatives. In particular, it raises questions about how we plan to understand individual responsibility and the ways in which one might treat (or punish) the person who does not make a choice in a difficult situation.

What about Griffin's claim that once one makes a choice in a perceived dilemma or any other case, comparability of some kind must be assumed. Griffin repeats that when a choice is forced on us we do prefer one option over another. We have reasons for our choice that allow for comparisons. But if I end up choosing in a situation that looks like a dilemma, is it perfectly transparent why I made my choice? What if I choose a less valued option because of certain anxieties felt in a given situation (something Griffin grants we might have in the case of autonomy)? Couldn't I also make a choice based on reasons that value my option but not necessarily over and above the other option?

Often we do just choose one thing because of its particular value, not because we have decided that it can be weighed against the value of other things. I may ponder a particular goal, serving the legal system as a public defender, and reject this, but not because the value it brings to me and/or society can be readily measured and compared to the more productive work I would do in biomedical research. The value of each end (assuming each is not only valuable to me but also to society in some way) is never easily determined in advance. I may simply choose based on the value of doing legal work as I believe that value is understood within our society (Raz 1986, ch. 13). Moreover, I may simply think that I could be more successful in one career over another. But even the potential for success could not be determined well enough in advance to allow for a firm ranking of sorts. Even this leaves us with a degree of indeterminacy. Add to this another point made by Raz about choice, that there may be "new beliefs acquired under the impact of the forced choice" that may have "changed these people's valuations rather than revealed them" (339), and we are rightly reminded that "rational action is action for (what the agent takes to be) an undefeated reason. It is not necessarily action for a reason which defeats all others" (339; also Lukes 1991, 48).

There is much to say about Griffin's second example and the comparisons between two artists with different goals. Griffin expects that overall goals (such as insight and being amused) can have comparative value "for us." The points just made, relying on Raz, indicate why the valued achievements of comprehensive goals may not always be readily compared, even when a choice is made. But in addition, Griffin's original example looks too easy. He asks us to compare the diverse achievements of two artists both of whom are writers. Alter the example slightly. Imagine a sculptor and a painter. Many would avoid saying that they can compare the value each artist offers and then determine which is better. Many would say, don't try to compare the goods promoted by these artists. If you want a well done abstract expressionist painting, assess this artist's work for A, B, and C reasons (related to the value of the art in the context of when it was done, what it was reacting to/against, how adeptly the artist uses colors, and so forth); or if you want a particularly powerful 20th century sculpture, look at this artist for these other reasons (having to do with certain points internal to the assessment of this particular artistic medium). We even seem unlikely to say that one artist, a poet considered less accomplished in her particular genre of writing, can be compared to a more successful or accomplished sculptor. More often than not we want to keep the assessment of each artist confined to criteria developed within the medium in which he or she operates. For all these problems, however, Griffin did compare the achievements associated with each artist in order to press his point (iii): that we mistake incommensurability for "rough equality." Even if we change Griffin's example about the artists above, he would still likely claim that even artists from different media are not totally incomparable.

Are we mistaking incommensurability for rough equality? Rough equality tells us that the gap between two values is not so great. But it also indicates that our choice between two options does not make a great deal of difference either, that one will be as good as the other—roughly the same. Is this, rather than incommensurability, often what we mean to say when trying to compare two valued ends or personality types? It seems clear that we care about our ends and perspectives, often for very distinctive reasons. Determining that a novelist with extraordinary insights and another with great humor are both good or promote valued ends, does not indicate that a choice between them makes little difference. To change the example slightly, imagine a writer at the end of a writing career and with limited time left to compose, trying to decide between pursuing his poetry or continuing original research into early American history. To say that the choice is not between terribly different ends—because the values to us seem about the same—may denigrate the impact the choice will have on the individual. To say that the choice is between incomparable options may convey something more accurate. It may tell us something about the weightiness and difficulty of choosing between two important options that have their own distinctive worth to the individual and perhaps to others.

Griffin's dismissal of Taylor's "incommensurably higher" values runs into similar difficulties. It ignores something important about a type of choice and the context in which individuals often refuse to make an exchange. Raz offers his own detailed discussion of the matter and presents several helpful examples. Imagine the case "of some parents who maintain that there is no way in which the value of having children can be compared with money, material position, status or prestige, etc. . . . . For such parents, having children and having money cannot be compared in value. Moreover, they will be indignant at the suggestion that such a comparison is possible. Finally, they will refuse to contemplate even the possibility of such an exchange" (Raz 1986, 346). Raz, as he often does, makes a reasonable qualification. "I deliberately hedge and refer to the attitude of some parents, since others may have perhaps superficially similar attitudes which none the less differ from the one I will use as an example of this kind of incommensurability" (346). But this does not dismiss the example; it only notes thoughtfully that not all "parents" are the same. Raz pursues other examples

Again, the incomparability of friendship and money in particular. Some "trade-offs involve a heavy price," and the willingness to refuse the trade-off is not a mistake or confusion.

Yet, many might respond by noting that a) even saying that one thing is more important than another, incommensurably higher as Taylor put it, commits us to making a comparison; or b) since we do often make trade-offs, even with important values, we admit that such values are ultimately exchangeable. But these points cannot explain away observations such as the following. First, we can put aside the term incommensurably "higher." This may have been a misplaced phrase or it may confuse the issue because in many cases we are not, as Taylor suggests, always talking about things that are "higher." We may want to highlight a finer or different distinction. As Raz admits, "keeping one's child is better than any amount of money, or anything that money can buy. I do not doubt that many do indeed hold that view. But my example concerns the others, those for whom it is equally unacceptable to buy a child as to sell one. For them it is not the case that having a child is worth more than any sum of money. If it were then they would not object to buying children when they want them" (347). Again, to ignore this is to "distort" some attitudes deserving of recognition. Not everyone will feel this way, but some will. Second, if we do make trade-offs involving a value we claim is incommensurable, this may not instantly imply that we rank, exchange or compare the value. "Many people . . . will leave their spouses for a month to do a job they do not like in order to earn some money," again Raz's example. "And yet they will not agree to leave the spouse for the same month for an offer of money, even a significantly larger sum of money. They will feel indignant that someone supposes that they are willing to trade the company of their spouse for money from a stranger." "Parting with one's spouse for a job, one is tempted to say, also means that in fact there is a price put on the company of one's spouse. But it does not have this symbolic significance (in the example above) and therefore is not perceived as equally objectionable" (349). We may compromise certain ends in the course of negotiating the complex demands of life. But we can engage in acts that show our on-going interest in promoting the incomparability of a value, even if the value seems compromised by other demands.

Even Griffin's final attempt to undermine the incommensurability resulting from the clash of two "world views" fails to dismiss these points. Griffin claims that we must eventually make a choice between world views when organizing our lives, and in so doing, we must rank. I have tried to suggest why this kind of argument is not always effective. In addition, Griffin suggests that clashes between two very distinctive world views are "rare." But can't incommensurability characterize those rare cases? In thinking about cultures across time, one might also find the term quite helpful (Williams 1985, ch. 9). No further reasons emerge in Griffin's final example to revise doubts about attempts to deny the incomparability. Situations likely will crop up where rankings or comparisons remain implausible or highly strained.

Overall, incommensurability in its strong forms and the pluralism it promotes may not, in all times and places, serve as a sign of great health and progress. Moreover, one is disinclined to trumpet the virtues of a concept that simply describes sharp differences, or that fails to generate the enthusiasm associated with legitimacy, freedom, or rights. However, the inclination to see incommensurability between groups within a culture as signifying moral decay and disorientation can and should be tempered. Moral incommensurability can serve as a precondition for other desirable commitments to the distinctiveness of competing values and virtues available to individuals who hope to choose from among many options when shaping their lives. Such a moral pluralism may not be valued in every society. But where it does exist, it need not lead to internal incoherence, a crude relativism, or become a condition simply to despise.

Three claims emerge here as relevant to this essay. First, moral incommensurability exists and is often associated with moral pluralism. Second, moral incommensurability is best understood in degrees. Third, those who dismiss moral incommensurability as severe and destructive of all equality talk, or else totally implausible, have work to do before their claims sound credible. We should explore a range of options for reaching across types of incommensurability. Options besides those offered by strong, liberal, and democratic egalitarians deserve attention and the next chapters build on this suggestion.

Notes

1. This stands in contrast to "American pluralism," for example. Though concerned with diversity, the latter has focused on what happens after "interests" are shaped by a group and the way groups interact within a "unified field" to "often engage in power struggles to define the directions of the field in which they coexist" (Rorty 1990, 7). Its main focus has been to portray "the system as a balance of power among overlapping economic, religious, ethnic, and geographic groupings. Each 'group' has some voice in shaping socially binding decisions; each constrains and is constrained through the process of mutual group adjustment; and all major groups share a broad system of beliefs and values which encourages conflict to proceed within established channels and allows initial disagreements to dissolve into compromise solutions" (Connolly, 1969, 3). Moral pluralism does have affinities with the above but can often refer to questions about how moral principles and even individual identities form and not only within "groups" but within interrelated, rule-governed practices or "ways of life."

2. We should also note that talk of incommensurability as I have pursued it does not simply refuse exploration about the construction of various common characteristics or values. Raz certainly avoids this as noted (1986, ch. 12). Stuart Hampshire, a thinker well-known for his relentless defense of moral pluralism and his critique of those "who look for an underlying harmony and unity behind the facts of moral experience" (1983 151) always assumes that values are formed within ways of life. "As thinking creatures we have to give meaning to our actions as satisfying certain descriptions, and there can

not be meaning without conventions" (1983, 148). Those who talk of incommensurability are not necessarily emotivists, to reiterate the obvious.

Moreover, Hampshire notes, in defense of his own position, that the kinds of arguments he makes about value conflicts (and those offered in a similar spirit) can avoid the "thesis that ways of life, with their priorities among virtues and their dependent moral rules, are not subjects for moral judgment, because there is no independent ground from which they can be evaluated. On the contrary," Hampshire claims, "there are several ways in which they can be judged and ought to be judged: not only may a way of life fail actually to satisfy the purposes, and to permit the virtues, which it purports to satisfy and to permit, and be internally incoherent; but it may also lead to the destruction of life and to greater misery" something that we can oppose based on certain shared concerns we may maintain about regard for the intelligence and physical integrity of persons and their need to be protected from harm at the very least (1983, 154). The stability of these boundaries and the very spartan notion of the person that they rest upon can run up against limits, especially if individuals consider their dignity and well-being closely bound up with the opportunity to choose potentially offensive goals (including goals that do involve harm to their own bodies). But nothing thus far would preclude all talk about such bounds (also see Hampshire 1989).

3. Fish criticizes Judith Butler, Chantal Mouffe, and Bonnie Honig as well (1999, 233-41; 131-42), though these thinkers might appear to be more consistent allies.

4. Valentine Moghadam makes this point well in the introduction to *Identity Politics and Women*. She tries to explore the politics and power surrounding "fundamentalist" religion in particular, so often pitted against western ideas and practices. Certain religious movements can be analyzed not simply as part of a different "culture" impenetrable to "our" moral point of view, but as themselves part of historical processes and contemporary developments, as sites within a society for contention between social groups and classes over economic resources and political power. Exploring this makes it much more difficult to label as illegitimate all "western" efforts to critique reassertions of tradition and cultural revival. (See Moghadam 1994, esp. 6-13.)

Chapter 5

Agency and Equal Regard

Earlier chapters criticized certain expectations about our capacity for autonomy and reviewed a range of contemporary thinkers who use such expectations to overcome moral differences and significant conflict. Chapter 4 added that the thinkers discussed should not be dismissed altogether; but if strong moral pluralism exists, then we may seek alternative characterizations of what we share. How should these alternatives look? My criticisms implicitly suggest the following: that talk about freedom should rest on a limited, spartan set of shared understandings, perhaps only on the expectation that everyone else should be free to pursue their own desires and be willing to treat others in instrumental terms, as bargainers with whom they must strike contingent agreements. Or else we might support a conservative anti-rationalism that eschews an "atomized" characterization of the self but leaves us bereft of reflective expectations and beholden to the traditions that deeply shape capacity for choice.

Neither of these would satisfy me, however. What is the alternative, then? One self-described conservative, Michael Oakeshott, has tried to clear a path out of this impasse with his eclectic characterization of freedom in relation to agency as opposed to autonomy and with his effort to promote what this chapter will call civil regard as opposed to respect for others.[1] I want to explore Oakeshott's ideas here, question some, and then build on others to establish my own alternative in chapter 6. The material of interest comes from the start of Oakeshott's 1975 *On Human Conduct*. Highly indebted to Hegel, Oakeshott tries to appreciate the way individuals are free only within the "goings-on" of life. But he also insists that as situated agents, individuals bring intelligence and even artistry to action. This requires a degree of self awareness, but not necessarily the critical reflection presupposed by autonomy. Oakeshott couples his observations with expectations about how individuals who live amidst rules and practices are never choked off from shaping the traditions that guide them and from demonstrating "virtuosity" alongside the expectations of shared norms. Agency looks highly accessible or inclusive in this rendition; it seems to strike the proper balance between describing individuals neither as self-interested bargainers nor as fully autonomous.

Moreover, while Oakeshott's characterization of agency may not incorporate expectations about an ability to transcend our differences or easily transform them, the (moral) expectations it does establish suggest that as interdependent language-users who demonstrate intelligence, we generally share the capacity to understand our world as we have created it through a context conditioned by the formal guidelines of rules and practices. Civil guidelines establish expectations for how to conduct ourselves, but these tend to let others pursue their own conceptions of the good. More often than not, we can share at least the capacity to follow civil "adverbial considerations" about how to act. When we do so moral differences are bridged, albeit in a chastened manner.

Oakeshott characterizes agents as both embedded yet equally capable of intelligent choice; able to reach out to others through common rules, yet still left to pursue their distinct goals. This approach also suggests that amidst conflicts marked by moral incommensurability, individuals can maintain coexistence even if consensus is less than feasible.

Attractions exist with Oakeshott. His expectations give shape to minimum conditions for equality and fair treatment of others. His requirements for what makes us similar are quite limited and formal. These ideas could fill out the continuum for addressing incommensurability as outlined briefly in chapter 4. But we should note that while these expectations may look well-suited to ameliorating strong moral incommensurability cautiously, they also appeal most when individuals are highly comfortable with, some might say complacent about, the traditions that shape conduct. Oakeshott's position depends upon confidence in the existing framework of our distinct language games, their formal character, and in a level of civility that may result only when both sides to a conflict can live with the idea of being left alone to maintain a certain status quo rather than promote more dramatic social change.

Appreciating Oakeshott's claims about agency, then, this chapter does go on to contest his position. In particular, I question Oakeshott's lack of attention to individual development within the "goings-on" of life. In order to remain capable of expressing "wished-for satisfactions," agents should be expected to scrutinize, with more informed historical astuteness, how and why the obligations and rules that bind them came into being. This need not be so terribly demanding an addition to Oakeshott's ideas. However, Oakeshott clearly would reject this direction. He insists that we put aside scrutiny of the "origins" of moral practices and the power that often shapes adverbial civil guidelines. But to ignore these points limits social change too dramatically or, worse, leaves open the potential to perpetuate oppression.

In the end, I highlight the value of Oakeshott's thinking, but modify his notion of agency and ethic of civil regard. I argue that the latter should be linked to an ethic of greater responsiveness toward agency development and differences in power that characterize many practices. The resulting discussion leads to chapter 6 where I modify a notion of agency more fully and link my ideas to the importance of "responsive regard" for others.

Oakeshott's Conservatism Reviewed

On Agency and Interdependence

Oakeshott's *On Human Conduct* begins with systematic discussions of how to "theorize" about agency.[2] In his effort to present two "postulates" of agency, Oakeshott makes clear that as active beings, humans remain capable of distinct wants and interests but these are situated in a world of "goings-on." They remain bound up with intelligent responses to already existing conditions. Oakeshott's first postulate of agency characterizes us as engaged in "doing, identified as response to a contingent situation related to an imagined and wished-for outcome." So, agents have desires (or, as Oakeshott puts it, "imagined and wished-for satisfactions") and these might be sources of motivation, but they are not brute urges. They are conditioned and prompt responses mediated by thought and choice. Agency also "postulates reflective consciousness." Our reactions involve choices based on reflections of "intelligible" goings-on, of situations learned and understood and inhabited by historically conditioned others. Our world is "composed of understandings" of potential performances (36).

Like many conservatives, Oakeshott is uninterested in how we stand as equals stripped down in a state of nature. Our distinctive goals and desires all take shape in a world of somethings rather than nothings for "us." Humans begin and remain in a state of interdependence; engagement in human conduct is never unencumbered.

Oakeshott says more about history and historical inquiry through other works (Oakeshott 1962; 1983). Of importance here is how the outset of *On Human Conduct* reinforces the role of a world prior to us; and while our past may not prescribe necessary substantive conditions or "the good life" that one must follow in the present, it establishes a web of shared languages and a host of events that "contingentially" relate to one another (1974, 94). Such practices may be neglected and change, but their features allow for a continuity rarely fully undone.

On Freedom as Intelligent Choice

These first postulates imagine us situated. We may make different choices, but qua humans we share the capacity for intelligent choice. What about the view of freedom implied here and its contrasts with others?

Oakeshott claims that "free agency" is rather "modest": "As a reflective consciousness [an agent's] situation is necessarily an understanding and as an understanding it is necessarily his own. He is '"free,"' Oakeshott believes, "not because his situation is alterable by an act of unconstrained 'will' but because it is an understood situation and because doing is an intelligent engagement. Nor does it matter how the agents have come by this understanding," Oakeshott continues, "because (since it is composed of beliefs) it cannot be a genetic inheritance, it cannot be the outcome of what has merely happened to him (what is sometimes miscalled his 'history') distinguished from his understanding of it, and it cannot have been imposed upon him by any external agency" (37). To make the point clearer:

> The 'freedom' intrinsic to agency is the independence enjoyed by the agent in respect of being a reflective consciousness composed of acquired feelings, emotions, sentiments, affections . . . etc., recognitions of himself and of the world of pragmata he inhabits, which he has turned into wishes, and wishes he has specified in choices of actions and utterances. It does not exclude him from giving reasons for what he has done or others from seeking them, for reasons are not causes and this freedom is not that of a so-called autonomous 'subjective will'. It does not depend upon his actions being 'rational' rather than 'emotional' responses. . . . It entails only the recognition of 'doing' as an intelligent engagement, action linked with learned and understood belief, distinguished from a genetic, a psychological, or a social process or from a consequence of causal conditions (40-41).

This suggests a picture of interdependence alongside independence. But in addition, agency cannot be described in terms of "organic conditions"—these make too little of the distinction between intelligent, learned conduct, and mere behavior. Freedom does not result because an individual is able to pursue certain processes associated with normal growth, eating, sleeping, and the like. *On Human Conduct* does not have Sen and Nussbaum in mind directly, but it critiques thinkers with similar inclinations, especially psychologists and economists of one sort or another.[3] True, Oakeshott writes, "there may be organic conditions which may make certain understandings less likely than others. A man congenitally deaf is not the most likely promoter of 'noise abatement' because he is not apt to recognize his own situation in terms of 'noise'. But his congenital condition does not exclude him from understanding his own situation in terms of 'noise', e.g.: 'I am the deaf husband of a wife who suffers greatly from the noise of air-traffic'" (37-38). An agent's "actions and utterances are the outcomes of what he (an agent) understands his situation to be," Oakeshott repeats, "and . . this understanding cannot be 'reduced' to a component of a genetic, a biochemi cal, a psychological or any other process, or to a consequence of any causal condition" (38).

The notion of individuals imagined free in terms of autonomy is eschewed as well. Free agency need not depend upon "'rational' rather than 'emotional' responses . . . wise rather than foolish, calculated to achieve their wished-for outcomes rather than impulsive" (40). These kinds of dichotomies depend upon "lonely" agents (79) "wholly responsible" for releasing themselves from impulses or desires by placing themselves under a command given by themselves to themselves in isolation (79). Better to recognize that "the self-understanding of the agent who is both the subject and the object postulated in conduct may be small, his powers of self-determination may be modest, he may be easily imposed upon, he may be duped into acting, but he is what he understands himself to be, his contingent situations are what he understands them to be, and the actions and utterances in which he responds to them are self-disclosures and self-enactments" (41). One might conclude that Oakeshott's description, in its own way, sees us as "lonely" free beings. But the point has limited impact given Oakeshott's respect for the "goings-on" that shape our imagination and wants. Oakeshott's additional rejection of utilitarianism takes the point further. For example, an individual "understanding his situation as that of being in debt and finding this unacceptable . . . recognizes himself to be invited to respond in an action or an utterance; he discloses in himself the character of an agent and acquires an employment. His situation is specific: he is not merely 'unhappy' or 'in pain', he is unacceptably in debt" (41). As such he (or she), even if shaped by "imagined and wished-for satisfactions," still understands his or her situation given the context of rules and norms. The ideal response to the indebtedness, noted above, may be "solvency or successful indifference to indebtedness" (42). But it still need not "prescribe any particular action to be performed." The agent will "choose what course of action he shall embark upon as a rejoinder to his situation" (42). These choices, even if an agent's own, "are not 'merely subjective': they are exhibitions of intelligence capable of being investigated" (52). "An action identified as a chosen response of an agent to a situation which he recognizes as his own does not postulate a self-absorbed agent incapable of understanding a situation other than in egocentric terms." An agent "may diagnose his situation as 'you are shivering' and he may himself respond accordingly. But self-reference (which is inherent) is not to be identified with self-preference" (52). "Or," to be more specific, "the spring of action cannot be understood as . . . I cannot want happiness; what I want is to idle in Avignon or to hear Caruso sing" (53).

A free agent has a "'history' but no 'nature'; he is what in conduct he becomes." When acting freely we do not transcend our context. History "is not an evolutionary or teleological process. It is what he [an agent] enacts for himself in a diurnal engagement, the unceasing articulation of understood response to endlessly emergent understood situations which continues until he quits the diurnal scene. And although he may imagine an 'ideal' human character and may use this character to direct his self-enactments, there is no ultimate or perfect man hidden in the womb of time or prefigured in the characters who now walk the earth" (41). In short, our freedom, relates to reflection composed of understandings of our world and, importantly, of understandings that need not converge upon "dispositions to act in a certain manner . . . nor subscription to the conditions of practices" (40-41).

But many will want to know why a situated agent is not obliged to do more than understand his or her context intelligently. Must we converge more fully with communal expectations? Do we ever critically evaluate rules?

In part these questions are addressed when Oakeshott's views of practices and rule following are given fuller expression.[4] Below I turn to this subject and then to the important questions just posed.

On Freedom, Rules, and the Artistry of Action

A practice, Oakeshott writes, "may be identified as a set of considerations, manners, uses, observances, customs, standards, canons, maxims, principles, rules, and offices specifying useful procedures or denoting obligations or duties which relate to human actions and utterances" (55). Oakeshott expects to balance freedom and self-expression alongside the collective constraints of a practice, however, by insisting on the following: a) any rules that shape us are a "continuously invented and always unfinished by-product of performances related to the achievement of imagined and wished-for satisfactions other than that of having a procedure" (56); b) the rules of a practice "can never tell a performer what choice he shall make; (they announce) . . . only conditions to be subscribed to in making choices" (58), hence the claim that "the requirements of a practice are not obeyed or disobeyed; they are subscribed to or not" (58); c) moral practices, unlike prudential ones, are devoid of attempts to actually achieve any substantive purpose even if they are born out of an effort to promote certain shared understandings (e.g., honesty is the best policy). "No doubt there may be advantages to be enjoyed in subscribing to its conditions. . . . But a moral practice, unlike an instrumental practice (one comprised of the rules for baking an angel food cake) does not stand condemned if no such advantages were to accrue" (60).

With these points, Oakeshott rounds out his discussion of agency. Appreciation for the historicity of individuals does not demand that conduct be constrained by substantive common ends. Oakeshott gets around the problem of how to support a strong sense of diversity alongside a situated notion of freedom and shared obligations because he believes that rules can (and should) be unconcerned with a "common good," a notion of the good life, higher-order human excellence and the like. Rules provide us with "adverbial considerations." They may be "concerned with good and bad conduct" (62), but "what they do is to concentrate into specific precepts considerations of adverbial desirability which lie dispersed in a moral language and thus transform invitations into prescriptions, allegiances to fellow practitioners into precise obligations" (66-67).[5] A moral practice and rules need never "constitute anything so specific as a 'shared system of values'; they compose a vernacular language of colloquial intercourse" (63). In so doing, they constitute an "art" or "an instrument which may be played upon with varying degrees of sensibility to its resources" (65). Individuals may be rule governed yet free.

On Civility and Our Common Vernacular

This description of agency is not devoid of ontological assumptions. So what does it get us? Oakeshott does not build a list of primary goods or necessary functionings from his notion of agency. Nor does he imagine appreciation for agency leading to mutual respect for others. Instead, we bridge differences via a "common vernacular." A rule-governed relationship in a moral practice deals with agents who share their relation to noninstrumental prescriptions.[6] What we "owe" others as equals might be described as a degree of civility—a sense that to act punctually, candidly, legally, rightly in each situation, is often the most we can ask for.

Oakeshott trims the demands placed on individuals in public life. In some ways, his efforts are not terribly distant from deliberate democrats whose notion of freedom leads to civil guidelines that shape deliberation and eventually transform differences. However, Oakeshott's expectations for others "like me" who fall under the jurisdiction of a rule are importantly different too. We all deserve to be recognized as rule-governed and treated equally under a rule; and in fact, Oakeshott admits that to the extent that individuals hope to act "publicly," it might be necessary that they "lose" their interest (170) in offering utterances "understood as awards of benefit or advantage to ascertainable individual or corporate interests" (168-69). But even this last point is described in terms of having a disciplined imagination not a deeper understanding of others. In other words, Oakeshott does not see deliberation between us, even in "politics," as a medium for transformation of our diverse perspectives. To recognize another as equal means we see that other as capable of an intelligent perspective with legitimate wants. This is not inconsequential. It makes it more difficult to exclude others or to dismiss them (uncivilly) as simply "blind religious fanatics," "dumb queers," "crazy feminists." But recognition and a full-blown version of respect may remain limited. Oakeshott asks others to control their demands and fulfill certain civil constraints; to advance proposals to accommodate a broad range of views (or advocate rules that seem as indifferent as possible). But, he is highly wary of anything more.

Conservative Dilemmas

Agency Development

Oakeshott's approach to free agency deserves a place among possibilities constructed here. On the one hand, Oakeshott's chastened description looks coherent and inclusive. On the other hand, it fails to discuss in enough detail how our capacity for intelligent choice and virtuosity should help develop and evaluate the rules around us. For Oakeshott, any critical assessment of rules must relate to the organic integrity of any rule-governed engagement. But in many cases, rules contributing to the "consistency" of a practice have been established through procedures that exclude or arrange competing demands in ways we would find unreasonable. Oakeshott resists talking about the origins of rules even as he briefly notes their need for evaluation (1983, 131). He says little about how some such responsive, evaluative capacity could contribute to being free and learning to sustain ourselves in ways that look mutually fair.

Of course, Oakeshott may deemphasize linking agency self-awareness to an evaluative process not because he believes "power" never exists or establishes unreasonable commands, but because he believes that the moral practices shaping us *ideally* should be devoid of instrumental power relations. Oakeshott makes this especially clear through consistent distinctions between what he calls moral conduct and transactional conduct. In transactional conduct, he writes,

> associates are known to each other solely as seekers of substantive satisfactions obtainable only in their responses to one another's conditional offers of satisfactions or threatened refusals to provide . . . sought-for satisfaction; and they are related in terms of their power to seek or to make such offers or to threaten or resist such refusals, and perhaps also in the recognition and use of such instruments (e.g. money), practices (e.g. promises) or maxims (caveat emptor) as they may have devised to promote the effective use of their power. Here, a bid in an auction sale and the patter of a salesman are exercises of power (1983, 122).

By contrast, moral conduct banishes functional or instrumental considerations from our binding habits. And Oakeshott adds that the practice of politics should do much the same. Commands associated with the "rule of law" stand for "a mode of moral association exclusively in terms of the recognition of the authority of known, non-instrumental rules . . . which impose obligations to subscribe to adverbial conditions in the performance of the self-chosen actions of all who fall within their jurisdiction" (1983, 136). The effort is instructive if one worries, as Oakeshott obviously does, about how a modern state tries to fulfill every need and establishes too many controversial interpretations of our shared ends. But for others, this is a worry taken to an extreme, leading to ideal distinctions that prize purity at the expense of all else.

Oakeshott would acknowledge his ideal tendencies. Part III of *On Human Conduct* indicates as much with its genealogy of the modern European state and its claim that constructions of the state as we know it have never been properly understood. To be more specific, Oakeshott argues that the European notion of the state went awry in the sixteenth century. The problem centers around two options, societas and universitas, which were both available for imagining how agents could relate to one another at the level of the state. Societas was preferable. But its importance became obscured.

> The idea of societas is that of agents who, by choice or circumstance, are related to one another so as to compose an identifiable association of a certain sort. The tie which joins them . . . is not that of an engagement in an enterprise to pursue a common substantive purpose or to promote a common interest, but that of loyalty to one another, the conditions of which may achieve the formality denoted by the kindred word 'legality.' Juristically, societas was understood to be the product of a pact or an agreement, not to act in concert but to acknowledge the authority of certain conditions in acting. . . . It was a formal relationship in terms of rule, not a substantive relationship in terms of action. But in the broader meaning (with which we are concerned) this constitutive pact became the description of an outcome: socii, each pursuing his own interests or even joined with some others in seeking common satisfactions, but related to one another in the continuous acknowledgment of the authority of rules of conduct indifferent to the pursuit or the achievement of any purpose. . . . It is what, in an earlier essay, I have called a moral relationship (1975, 201-202).

Universitas, on the other hand, stood for a corporate association "recognized (by Roman jurists) as persons associated in respect of some identified common purpose, in the pursuit of some acknowledged substantive end, or in the promotion of some specified enduring interest" (203). Not surprisingly, Oakeshott identifies the latter conception with "the tireless extension and elaboration of a central apparatus of ruling"—and with "exploitation of resources," "subjects as role performers" (268 and 269) and with the "individual manqué" who looks for a patron (rather than someone in authority) to fulfill needs and act as the promoter of desirable substantive outcomes. Oakeshott sees the (modern) world consumed by universitas. The societas with its proper cultivation of a civil association is nowhere to be found. Hence, the insistence on a degree of purity, as I have called it. If we had sustained the purposeless view of moral and legal rules noted, we might never have needed the scrutiny mentioned, or at least not the level of evaluation of rules that still seems important to agency. Rules properly understood would never fall prey to instrumental concerns or unreasonable impositions.[7] And rules properly understood would have left us with enough freedom to instigate change gradually and prevent unfair exclusions.

But even if we grant the conceptual distinctions (between societas and universitas, civil and enterprise associations, commands of an economic exchange and prescriptions of a "game" like chess), Oakeshott would need to maintain these distinctions. And he admits, sustaining his ideal categories has never come easily. So why drain free agency of a more scrutinizing capacity? Such scrutinizing will not require divorcing oneself from current practices altogether. On the contrary, one will likely need to be fully engaged and active as a participant hoping to alter specific arrangements. But if alterations are needed and require the intelligent understanding Oakeshott values, they also require the courage to question, probe, and provide resources in ways responsive to the very different voices that participate in rules over time.

One might go further and note the difficulties that exist imagining any society where talk of power is so divorced from public interactions. A more effective effort to promote free agency and fair rules would acknowledge the ongoing interaction between moral and transactional associations, societas and universitas. We could modify Oakeshott's position even more dramatically, then. Any role established by certain rules requires adherence to numerous formal adverbials—for example, a teaching post may require arriving punctually, grading fairly, or dressing cleanly and professionally. These formal adverbials might provide several shared expectations. But it should be possible to acknowledge how dressing "cleanly and professionally" (and/or perhaps in a "lady-like" way as a teacher) has been developed by certain people, at a certain time and for certain reasons. Some may believe that any mention of dress codes or physical hygiene is irrelevant to the stated purpose of teaching, or that the way these obligations have developed is objectionable given the current demands of the classroom. These questions might be posed by any generation in any number of ways. But it will be important to trace a history of who established these requirements and why; whether they remain open to review; and whether the men and/or women who established them can explain what made and still makes their ideas relevant. Why should relevance only be determined by whether a rule is faithful or "authentic" to the practice, as Oakeshott claims? And aren't we frequently debating key characterizations of good teaching? Aren't the key substantive purposes of any practice (rightfully) often up for debate? It will not be easy to see agents as free if they fail to have the capacity to pose such questions assuming that power always has some role in the construction of rules.[8]

Oakeshott has said that the "stories" that bind us, that tell us who we are and where we come from, are not properly constructed with introductions such as "in the beginning." They start with "once upon a time" (1975, 105). This is to suggest that our current understandings are closer to legends with mysterious pasts that we interject ourselves into even though we cannot pinpoint their origins. But even as this observation accounts for the continuity of history and the contextual character of occurrences, even as it looks properly skeptical of an "original occurrence in terms of which all subsequent occurrence may be understood," (104) it seems unaware of how the "invitations" to venture into a "response" to what has come before may not be perfectly recognizable or perfectly civil. They may be angry complements rather than gentle maneuvers, something odd or striking and perhaps not readily identified as "holding together" (104) with what surrounds it. We will want or need to criticize more fully what has come before. And that may unsettle the delicate web of shared understandings.

In earlier writings, such as "The Rule of Law," Oakeshott hints about further opportunities for evaluating rules. He writes at one point: "Nevertheless, rules may also be appreciated in respect of what they prescribe. This is what must occupy the attention of the makers of rules and it may be the legitimate concern of others. Since what a rule prescribes is an obligation to subscribe to non-instrumental adverbial conditions in the performance of the self-chosen actions of all who fall within its jurisdiction, what fails to be appreciated here is the actual conditions it obligates them to observe. Among makers of rules this may invoke a variety of prudential and consequential considerations (such as the difficulty or probable cost of detecting a delinquency) but for them and for others its central concern is with what may be called, somewhat loosely, the 'evaluation' of these conditions distinguished from the determination of their authenticity" (1983, 130-31). This seems to value more room for critical maneuvering. But such hints are much less notable in the magnum opus *On Human Conduct*. With the latter as Oakeshott's formidable guide, we can only wonder how far this approach goes toward rule evaluation and just how far we can raise our voices to probe and interpret quite differently without being seen as unreasonably disruptive.

On Responsiveness and Concern for Others

I have raised concerns about Oakeshott's construction of agency and its expectations about how we develop capacities to evaluate our freedom in relation to existing practices. Let me now make some remarks about the capacity of civility. I want to ask again whether Oakeshott goes far enough toward inclusiveness and specifically whether civil regard prompts appropriate and fair review of how others can use the adverbials that inform a practice. This has some links to the points just made above. But it gets at a slightly different concern.

Even in the face of distinct differences, we may be able to remain civil. But civility, as Oakeshott conceives of it, does not press us to listen and carefully examine the conditions that have led us to understand how we now use certain rules. As I see it, we can and should show civil regard for others but also demonstrate greater care and concern about the world we share even amidst our significant diversity. We can and should do this because as interconnected beings we should also feel responsibility for the rules all benefit from and try to live by. This responsibility can only be demonstrated through an attitude of responsiveness that takes civility seriously but adds to it a willingness to look at, or show concern about, and act upon, the implications rules have for others.

Oakeshott does not pursue these additional expectations as they may push for more virtuous demands and imply far too much about how well we can understand and presume to speak on behalf of others. This last issue is tackled in the next chapter. But, as an aside, I should note that although I have criticized positions, like Martha Nussbaum's, for supporting a particular version of positive freedom and for maintaining set lists of needs or necessary capabilities,

Oakeshott's position goes to the other extreme. It becomes so enamored of formal rules and so resistant to seeing a properly governed, civil society infected by instrumental concerns, that it rarely tries to imagine any further supporting structures and attitudes necessary for rule use and civil conduct. Again, Oakeshott never considers identifying (or legitimating the process of identifying) resources that will make self-guiding individuals capable of project pursuits in particular practices. One need not compile overarching, general lists to get at this issue. We could say that when the formal conditions of this or that workplace X are identified, we will expect various goods a, b, and c will facilitate an individual's capacity to have access to and use of the rules that characterize the practice. To a significant extent, this approach is suggested by Michael Walzer's discussion of the plurality of social goods needed in different "spheres" of conduct. Oakeshott simply ignores these approaches. Presumably individuals learn slowly how to act punctually, vigorously, prudentially, generously, etc., and they learn how to perform or meet an obligation in better or worse ways. It is not unfathomable that the "things" needed to bolster learning how to perform well could be identified and remain "internally consistent" with our understandings of the obligations prescribed by a practice. I agree that we can find competing interpretations of what individuals "need" when learning how to perform or understand obligations in any particular situation (just as there will be competing interpretations of which rules should be applied when). But the point ignored by Oakeshott is that we may need to deal in some way with the distribution of material resources in order to "play" the non-instrumental games valued. More substantive considerations will need attention if freedom is the desired goal.

Oakeshott offers a helpful description of agency, rules, and civility. However, while putting together an important alternative, Oakeshott's expectations about social stability and his complacency about the need for social change pose limits. His position cannot (like its deliberative democratic counterpart) remain unaware of other alternatives. In many cases, we would do well to continue thinking about ways to characterize agency to promote equality. The last chapter aims to do this and it moves toward another complementary approach to the problem at hand.

Notes

1. Also see Kukathas (1992) for another effort to shift to talk about agency, this time in contrast to William Kymlicka's liberal view of autonomy (1989).

2. Here is how Oakeshott begins to discuss what it means to theorize about human conduct and agency. "To be human and to be aware is to encounter only what is in some manner understood. Thus, it may be said that understanding is an unsought condition; we inexorably inhabit a world intelligible. But understanding as an engagement is an exertion; it is the resolve to inhabit an ever more intelligible, or an ever less mysterious world

This unconditional engagement of understanding I shall call 'theorizing'. It isn't engagement to abate history rather than to achieve definitive understanding" (1975, 1).

3. Unless otherwise indicated, citations throughout the chapter refer to pages in *On Human Conduct*.

3. It is also interesting to compare how Nussbaum reads Aristotle differently than Oakeshott. See his 1975 n.1, 118.

4. As should be clear, even though I take issue with conservative elements in Oakeshott, he has, nonetheless, tempered his links to certain (communitarian-like) expectations through his formal view of rule following with its focus on supporting a high degree of self-expression alongside an appreciation for collectively constructed practices.

5. These comments also influence the more explicit discussions of citizenship and politics found in OHC. Oakeshott talks about moral rules qua laws (or lex). Such rules are more abstract, yet more exact manifestations of moral rules. Lex joins "strangers" as "equals." And individuals who fall under a rule's jurisdiction "are equal in respect of the rule" (125). Lex, of course, does not demand that its users achieve certain ends even though it prescribes "common responsibilities and rights." And while open to on-going contestation and reevaluation in political deliberation, even rules of law cannot be put forward in order to further certain powerful interests over others, certain specific ends that result from "bargaining." It is again the case that moral rules appropriate to a formal association (in this case a practice that Oakeshott calls civil association) can join us without demanding certain onerous limits. While lex is a more specific form of rule-following, identified with cives or citizens, it is indebted to the characterization of our relationship as equals in terms of moral rules as described above. There are, of course, many prudential transactions occurring between individuals, Oakeshott notes, and the rules of prudential practices may well be instrumental to satisfying some common satisfaction that individuals come to agree upon.

6. In a moral practice, for example, there is "a relationship of equals not because all users of a language are equally competent but because they are all concerned with the same skill and are specified in the same terms: a relation of flute-players, not of flute-players to audiences; of French-speakers in respect of their language, not in respect of what they have to say" (1975, 121). A relation in terms of lex takes this one step further: the "instrument" of civil conversation "in which agents recognize and disclose themselves as cives" (as formal equals in the broadest sense) becomes lex because rules become a "self-sufficient system" where a legislative process enacts rules for all, where cives continue to deliberate over the "desirability" of such rules, and where an adjudicative procedure amplifies the meaning of rules by applying them in various unforeseen circumstances. Lex is never perfectly systematic. And it never derives its validation from one ultimate rule or source. But it is recognized as the proper association for joining strangers perhaps even more distant from each other than those occupying roles in a host of other moral associations. It expects the understanding of rules developed throughout moral life to now carry over, albeit in a more strictly formal way, into governing the life of a state (or ideal societas).

7. Comparisons with Hannah Arendt's noninstrumental vision of politics are intriguing to explore. See Arendt 1959.

8. Nancy Fraser adds to these reminders with her criticisms of Habermas' distinctions (1989, ch. 6) and her efforts to remind thinkers, not unlike Oakeshott, that "in the capitalist marketplace, for example, strategic, utility maximizing exchanges occur against a horizon of intersubjectively shared meetings and norms; agents normally subscribe at least tacitly to some commonly held notion of reciprocity and to some shared conceptions about the social meaning of objects, including what sorts of thing are considered ex-

changeable. Similarly, in the capitalist workplace, managers and subordinates, as well as coworkers, normally coordinate their actions to some extent consensually and with some explicit or implicit reference to normative assumptions, though the consensus be arrived at unfairly and the norms incapable of withstanding critical scrutiny. Thus the capitalist economic system has a moral-cultural dimension.

Likewise, few if any human action contexts are wholly devoid of strategic calculation. Gift rituals in noncapitalist societies, for example, previously taken as a veritable crucible of solidarity, are now widely understood to have a significant strategic, calculative dimension, one enacted in the medium of power if not that of money. And as I shall argue in more detail later, the modern restricted nuclear family is not devoid of individual, self-interested, strategic calculations in either medium (118)." The continuation of Fraser's discussion here buttresses these points.

Chapter 6

Toward Responsive Regard

This chapter aims to reconsider equality in relation to appreciation for and protection of agency. It couples this with an equality ethic called responsive regard. These suggestions emerge through negotiations with earlier thinkers. My ideas stand especially indebted to and antagonistic toward Oakeshott and deliberative democrats. I modify Oakeshott's conception of agency using insights from Susan Brison (1997) and Drucilla Cornell (1995, 1997), the latter being particularly concerned about criticizing and recasting equality while responding to feminist skepticism about the concept. In the end, I suggest agency as I describe it remains situated but chastened enough to be broadly inclusive in certain diverse climates. It can and should provide general expectations for encouraging civility and limiting efforts to degrade or silence others during public exchange. And it can support certain provisions for substantive equal opportunities, thereby dealing with concerns about distributive and not only (as Nancy Fraser (1997) puts it) cultural justice.

In the end, positions reviewed earlier could remain more or less desirable depending upon the level of moral pluralism expected or wanted in a society. A register of possibilities should be available, although I will be arguing that interest in strong moral pluralism and fairness makes the protections offered by my conception of agency, as well as the room it carves out for political action through "crossover coalitions" and responsive regard, distinctly attractive.

Agency Reconsidered

As agents humans are purposive actors as well as intelligent language users capable of understanding how to disclose themselves and "go on" within the rules of various practices. We can and should be considered equals to the extent that, at the very least, we all form desires but also remain capable of the "virtuosity" needed to pursue "wished for satisfactions," as Oakeshott puts it, something which involves learning to maneuver amidst the formal linguistic guidelines of traditions and local languages. Virtuosity requires some general education and demonstrations, then; it requires access to the artistry of existing norms. But because these expectations for action can remain modest and often formal, the conditions for promoting agency should not force rigid conformity to particular ends; they can look particularly sensitive to diverse interests and futures.

Oakeshott helped conceptualize this view in chapter 5. The position avoids difficulties associated with strong egalitarians related to their more demanding form of positive freedom. It does not reject efforts to describe postulates of "human" conduct (perhaps because the notion of agency makes more modest demands), and as a result, it does not face some of the internal vacillations confronted by political liberals. Finally, it talks of situated, rule-governed agency leading to collective understandings about how agents should approach others who deserve the opportunity to pursue their own plans. The approach expects a web of linguistic bridges to emerge between us, similar to the civil speaking and acting that deliberative democrats advocate. But this can be done without some of the controversies of deliberative "reciprocity." A political theory committed to protecting this view of agency leads to a kind of civil regard for others that allows for coexistence but limits the characterological transformation required by deliberative democrats.

However, there is more to add. Agency remains a potentiality, not a taken for granted condition, and Oakeshott fails to recognize this fully. Keeping in mind my concerns about practices and their relation to agency as discussed in chapter 5, I wish to link support for agency to an acknowledgment that individuals with situated, wished-for satisfactions are only capable of "going on" and acting freely when protected from loss of physical integrity as well as self-esteem.

I need to defend why such a filled out description of freedom can avoid becoming too perfectionist-oriented and distinguish itself from elements in the strong equality position. Simultaneously, I want to avoid reenacting political liberalism's preoccupation with eschewing all general assumptions about human psychological or moral development or the role played by the family in developing freedom-related capacities.

To find a proper description balancing these concerns I lay out thoughts here about physical integrity and self-esteem. I present these as commonsensical additions to a vision of agency. I buttress my points by turning to Susan Brison's discussion on trauma and identity. I also explore Drucilla Cornell's ideas about protection of "psychic space" and the "imaginary domain." The sections below fill out a conception of agency using Brison and Cornell's insights without unconditionally championing one school of psychology. But I implicitly suggest we take seriously the "testimony" from which these points are drawn and, in so doing, recognize that such testimony may not provide a specific, well-grounded list of common ends to pursue, but rather a set of tentative limits to take seriously wherever the equality of agency is valued.

Agency, Integrity, and Self-Esteem

What is meant by emphasizing protection of physical integrity seems obvious. It is perhaps best explained in relation to what it is not. Humans lack physical integrity, and therefore a fully functioning capacity for agency, when subjected to assaults on the body, when facing certain physical obstacles and impositions that produce physical helplessness and impede the pursuit of chosen purposes.

We need not, however, restrict ourselves to this claim based on what we see on the outside of the body as when we view persons subject to torture or physical coercion. The emotional effects brought about by physical assaults, even if not causing death, are often significant. Here Susan Brison's explorations of trauma look astute. Even if a harm causing fear or a significant threat can be removed, its effects on mental perceptions and other inner states can remain to diminish self-esteem, leading many to confront additional obstacles to projecting future goals or knowing how to go on.

Recognizing this leads to another point. Some would say that if we can link a sense of physical integrity to avoidance of certain mental or emotional hindrances, why not try to protect against the latter even before bodily violations occur? In other words, as someone like Cornell could put it, why not attend to degradation of "psychic space" in its own right? This "space" enables projection of a future and goes to the heart of agency and action.

As I see it, protecting physical integrity involves attending to both external and internal attributes. With respect to the latter, I would highlight the importance of self-esteem, however, rather than psychic space.[1] As I see it, self-esteem refers to a dignified feeling of value from within, to a capacity to regard the self as worthy of having purposes, as having a certain authenticity and loyalty to its own choices. Without this, without insuring at least a chance to maintain self-esteem, personal goals look decidedly more difficult to dream about let alone pursue. The question is, what are the implications of integrating this concern about self-esteem into talk about agency and the need for protections against violations of physical integrity.

We can turn to Brison first simply to reinforce the initial point, that experiencing bodily harm affects us psychologically even after significant physical threats subside. Certain violations leave powerful marks; so do fears. Although I consider it worthy to protect self-esteem and to highlight its importance as a limiting condition, I also recognize the potential dangers in doing this. Nonetheless, I expect to take these concerns into account while still showing attention to moral pluralism and freedom.

To begin, let me return to Brison. As a philosopher but also someone traumatized through devastating sexual assault, Brison explores the complex "undoing of the self" following loss of physical integrity. She takes care not to overshadow broader philosophical discussion with her own injuries, but her "testimony" does weave itself into observations; and she offers noteworthy points about how bodily violations disrupt a range of perceptions about how one can go on or retain purpose in life. Pursuing her investigations, Brison categorizes mental states creating a web of obstacles to reasonably effective agency.

The first such state has to do with the distance or dissociation from the body often described in the wake of violent acts. These produce difficulties for relocating oneself within the world, for situating oneself in any reasonably comfortable way, after violence has occurred. Brison talks about herself, as well as others, who have experienced war, torture, and concentration camps. "The study of trauma does not lead to the conclusion that the self can be identified with the body, but it does show how the body and one's perception of it are nonetheless essential components of the self. It also reveals the ways in which one's ability to feel at home in the world is as much a physical as an epistemological accomplishment" (1997, 18). Brison goes on to cite Jean Amery's discussion of torture and how the one who is tortured

> from the moment of the first blow . . . loses 'trust in the world,' which includes 'the rational and logically unjustifiable belief in absolute causality perhaps.'. . . More important, according to Amery, is the loss of the certainty that other persons 'will respect my physical, and with it also my metaphysical, being. The boundaries of my body are also the boundaries of myself. My skin surface shields me against the external world. If I am to have trust, I must feel on it only what I want to feel. At the first blow, however, this trust in the world breaks down' (18).

Like a character living in Hobbes's state of nature, the individual here loses the sense of physical integrity, a sense that he or she can settle into the world. Such a body may not remain under direct physical assault, but its continued perception of reduced security limits chances to settle into its skin and heightens fear of death.

Brison also notes how adult victims of rape "report the kind of splitting from their bodies during the assault, as well as a separation from their former self in the aftermath of the rape. Several months after the sexual assault and murder attempt I survived, I felt as though I had out lived myself, as though I had stayed on the train one stop past my destination" (19). Survivors of concentration camps often give themselves new names after their release. These mechanisms, too, help people go on. But the mechanisms may demonstrate, again, that

> these responses to trauma—whether dissociation from one's body or separation from the self that one was either before or during the trauma—have in common

the attempt to distance one's (real) self from the bodily self that is being degraded, and whose survival demands that one do, or at any rate be subjected to,
degrading things. But such an attempt is never wholly successful, and the survivor's bodily sense of self is permanently altered by an encounter with death
that leaves one feeling 'marked' for life (20).

We may be situated in a world, but a situated self may be disrupted dramatically. We may learn how to "go on" within a practice, but learning can be up-
rooted. Ways exist to recapture connections, but we should also protect individuals against the emotional disruptions that we know can create trauma.
Again, the capacity for agency and its development cannot be taken for granted.

Some would say that dissociated trauma survivors discover ways to go on by
constructing new stories, by placing their experience within a larger narrative.
As one reconceives of oneself, one integrates the traumatic episode into one's
overall life story, into a present with a past. But how to accomplish this? Brison
cites Charlotte Delbo to reinforce how memory fragmentation when taken too
far presents significant difficulties even for formulating intelligible purposes.
Delbo, a former concentration camp inmate, writes about how "the survivor
must undertake to regain his memory, regain what he possessed before: his
knowledge, his experience, his childhood memories, his manual dexterity and
his intellectual faculties, sensitivity, the capacity to dream, imagine, laugh" (Brison 1997, 20, citing Delbo). Delbo recalls after her initial release asking herself
odd questions too: "Had I a former life? My life afterwards? Was I alive to have
an afterwards to know what afterward meant? I was floating in a present void of
reality" (23, citing Delbo). Others note their dilemmas with memory loss or
changes in perception of time. "We had not only forgotten our country and our
culture, but also our family, our past, the future we had imagined for ourselves,
because, like animals," wrote Primo Levi, "we were confined to the present
moment" (22-23, citing Levi).

A community of survivors may be needed to witness one's perceptions and
reintegrate memory. One may also need to share stories with those distanced
from one's experience in order to find broader solidarity and help build protests
against future harm. "The truth is that to grasp the Holocaust whole-of-horror is
not to comprehend or transcend it," writes Emile Fackenheim, "but rather to say
no to it, or resist it" (Fackenheim cited in Brison 30-31). And Brison writes
about this effectively, again citing her own experience. "When I was hospital-
ized after my assault I experienced moments of reprieve from vivid and terrify-
ing flash backs when giving my account of what happened—to the police, doc-
tors, a psychiatrist, a lawyer, and prosecutor. Although others apologized for
putting me through what seemed to them a re-traumatizing ordeal, I responded
that it was therapeutic, even at that early stage, to bear witness in the presence of
others who heard and believed what I told them" (Brison 1997, 23).

Having a chance to survive, think back, and construct a story that others
want to hear may not require a view of memory and tradition modeled by communitarian writers of late. Charles Taylor's approach to retrieving our history

has been mentioned already and its problems noted. My points should highlight, at the very least, the value of avoiding a reduction in one's ability to imagine a future. How we reconstruct the past and link it to the present and future may differ; how we envision and pursue a "life plan" may vary; whether or not we connect the story to a shared sense of value from the past is up for debate. Nonetheless, in many circumstances, we can do something more limited; we can identify obstacles to constructing memories and we can try to prevent them.

One final difficulty often faced after trauma relates to an individual's capacity to function as a subject of action. Dramatic loss of control over one's physical environment, coupled with treatment as a thing, a number, something to be exploited, heightens the perception that one remains an object upon which others act rather than someone with a will to exercise. As a result, Brison writes that, "it is not sufficient for mastering trauma to construct a narrative of it: one must (physically, publicly) say or write (or paint or film) the narrative, and others must see or hear it, in order for one's survival as autonomous self to be complete" (29). One may depend upon others to help facilitate a sense of control and decisiveness. But one must regain an internal sense of acting as a subject even if this requires some accommodations from or interdependence with others. Again Brison: "in the year after my assault, when I was terrified to walk alone, I was able to go to talks and other events on campus by having a friend walk with me. I became able to use the locker room in the gym after getting the university to put a lock on the door that led to a dark, isolated passage way, and I was able to park my car at night after lobbying the university to put a light in the parking lot" (28).

One maintains agency by avoiding attacks on the body, and avoiding sustained fears that hinder action even after attacks cease. Certain fears degrade our connection to others or reduce our ability to participate in and create stories that provide for meaningful futures. Acknowledging this does not immediately prescribe how to connect to others, create narratives, participate as a subject. But we can say that several inner states remain linked to outer conditions that dramatically limit life planning. We can place a higher-order value on such avoidance. To say this much is not insignificant.

Critics could voice two complaints. First, these gestures look too limited. Second, these assumptions demonstrate too much assurance regarding the human psyche—and, perhaps, show an unwitting inclination to replicate another list of necessary goods or functionings as the prerequisite for maintaining agency (something I found troublesome in earlier chapters). I could respond to the first concern by presenting examples below about how protecting self-esteem can lead to further substantive concrete implications. I could respond to the second concern by reiterating how any examples elaborating on the application of this idea need not depend upon a set list so much as a set of limiting conditions and protections applicable to specific situations. Moreover, I would add another point. A thinker like Oakeshott is most likely to resist adopting these additional observations; but, I believe that Oakeshott's own conception of self-enactment lends support to the direction I take. Self-enactment, which Oakeshot explores as necessary for understanding agency, is not quite self-esteem as defined here, but it has affinities with the latter. Although the more insistent minimalist in this discussion, even Oakeshott would need to acknowledge the importance of the direction I have promoted.

Protecting Agency

Let me pull together some thoughts. Elements of the view of agency discussed in chapter 5 remain attractive but only 1) if our analysis of rules, and the notion of how they situate us, attend to concerns about power and 2) if access to practices and use of adverbial considerations require protection against diminished abilities to imagine and pursue purposes that define the exercise of agency. I have gone further with point 2) and claimed that protection should involve attention to physical integrity as well as self-esteem. But how far should we take this last concern about self-esteem? What happens when physical violence is not yet obvious but threats to self-esteem have occurred and need to be limited? What kinds of situations could these include? How can we balance concerns about self-esteem alongside conflicting forms of individual expression?

Let me turn again to some examples, ones that present difficulties because they demonstrate tension between trying to show concern about self-esteem yet protect free speech. Over the past decade many college campuses have struggled with speech codes. If we value choice and individual agency, many such codes look troublesome. But if we share concern about the demoralizing affects on those who must listen to or watch the speech or symbols associated with groups that have a history of hate and even violence, allowing certain displays unsettles. Efforts to address this issue can tend toward an either/or situation: straight liberal rejection of such codes or demands for moral reprimands, even coupled with sensitivity education for offending speakers. My inclinations look suited to a liberal free speech defense (assuming we are referring to speech not directly linked to inciting violence). However, the speech of concern here often targets some as unworthy and unwelcome within the community, possibly creating fear of attack via the inclination to degrade and dehumanize. What can the concern about self-esteem say about this?

Some speech or symbols or actions offend; others are directed toward making us feel like objects of attack or ridicule and rejection as persons. Certain forms of speech likely to produce the latter seem worth challenging given my point about self-esteem and its relation to fears about harm and integrity. The fears engendered by speech would have to be significantly degrading given a particular context—and often even this kind of speech should not be simply censored outright. But we can ask that it be evaluated or tempered, that it be recognized as causing degradation and that it be discussed as such.

Take complaints about inviting a known anti-Semitic speaker to campus or allowing someone to hang a confederate flag outside a dorm room for display

onto a public lawn. These seem especially prone to increasing fear and provok-
ing hostility. It may not look desirable to stifle or morally reorient individuals
engaged in such conduct. We often have to live with speech as well as symbolic
action we find near intolerable. But we may not wish to stop here even if violence has yet to erupt. It remains troublesome to see any institution with a diverse array of individuals remain indifferent to the speech or symbols in question. Although we may wish to honor the first amendment, why should general
rules governing all of us as agents implicitly support controversial conduct by
doing and saying nothing in response? The institution finding an anti-Semitic
speaker in its midst might make it possible for those who oppose the speaker to
pursue various tactics for protest. Petitions might be sent to the group that spon-
sored the event to demonstrate some level of disdain or revulsion; requests
might be made to avoid having the sponsoring campus group present the speaker
without any challenging rebuttal, or the campus organization sponsoring the
event might be asked not to use collective funds to host this speaker. In the case
of the flag, confiscation would be extreme, as would the demand that the owner
of the flag attend something like sensitivity training. But rules addressing the
issue could insist that no such symbols be displayed on the facade of a shared
building, that no one should be forced to view the symbol which so many associate with recent degradation; and that if somebody wishes to display it, it must
remain within the confines of a room clearly identifiable with the individual who
endorses and takes responsibility for its message.

Different ways exist to address these examples, but we can protest and protect against the fears these images evoke, fears that may not outweigh free
speech completely, but fears related to our concerns about self-esteem and the
ways in which these relate to individuals' ability to imagine themselves as acknowledged equals deserving the chance to have purposes and, like others, exercise agency as fully as possible.

Drucilla Cornell helps expand on this point. Her recent works focus on developing a concept of equality and this in response to feminists highly skeptical
of the concept (1997; 1995; 1992b). Cornell has used an appreciation for free
and equal personhood to defend new approaches to abortion, pornography, and
sexual harassment. I support a more cautious conception of agency in contrast
with Cornell's notably Rawlsian liberal conception of personhood and autonomy. I would claim that my notion of agency can prove more conducive to the
message Cornell wants to convey. For the moment, however, let me simply
draw upon one of Cornell's examples to show another application of my ideas.
Cornell's response to pornography regulations has interesting affinities with the
argument thus far.

Pornography may degrade and lower the self-esteem of certain individuals
who see it. But shouldn't someone who values freedom and the equal opportunity to pursue even eccentric or offensive purposes resist regulating pornography? Isn't defining the term pornography an issue that makes regulation difficult? Putting aside debate over this last point, let's say that we can define pornographic material and that Cornell's attempt to do so sounds acceptable. Cornel'

defines the pornographic as "explicit presentation and depiction of sexual organs and sexual acts with the aim of arousing sexual feeling through either a) the portrayal of violence and coercion against women as the basis of heterosexual desire or b) the graphic description of woman's body as dismembered by her being reduced to her sex and stripped completely of her personhood as she is portrayed in involvement in explicit sex acts" (Cornell 1995, 106). How can concern about self-esteem as well as physical integrity let us ignore this?

My approach to agency should not allow for indifference here. But regulating images requires caution. Taking on the forceful analysis and efforts to regulate pornography developed by Katharine MacKinnon, Cornell also recognizes the validity of a woman's demand not to be "an enforced viewer of pornography." But she rejects seeing pornography and the fantasies it plays upon as a type of coercive speech and worth regulating as such. Viewing pornography does not create the same degradation, for example, as a sign one might see on an employer's door that says "Whites Only." In trying to analyze the distinction between pornographic imagery and the "whites only" sign, Cornell observes how

> that sign is a form of action in that there can be no possibility of employment of blacks in that workplace. Of course, who is doing the communicating through the sign is also crucial. An employer has the power to keep blacks out by refusing to even interview them, let alone hire them. Thus, we clearly need to separate a sign on the door of a place of employment from someone walking down the street screaming, "no whites may apply." The fact that the "speaker" is an employer is inseparable from the coercive affect of the words. Coercive speech acts, then, not only imply the meaning given to the words, they also imply the force needed to make them an actuality. Given the history of exclusion, the sign clearly enacts the discrimination against which Title VII and the Constitution are meant to protect. But since pornography does not and cannot speak directly if it is to continue to be arousing, do we want to give it the kind of power that a "whites only" sign has to effectuate discrimination in its very expression when it is placed on the door of a place of employment? The answer has to be both a political and a legal one. Politically, we must not grant pornography the power to coerce women through its substitution for reality. To do so is to insert ourselves back into the pornographic worldview in which men's actions effectively curtailed women in their expression and in their search for new affirmation of the feminine within sexual difference beyond any current definitions. Simply put, we are not their fantasies. We do not want to have the law recognize their fantasies as the truth of our "being." It gives pornography too much power to argue that it effectuates and enacts subordination through its very existence (1995, 143).

Politically, protests against pornography are in order. It is worth encouraging those who work within the porn industry to unionize and protest work conditions. But legally, why validate that pornography tells "the truth" about women?

So should any images or speech defined as pornographic be regulated? One answer essentially comes back to my discussion about self-esteem. We should acknowledge the problematic expectations about women that pornography projects. But these must be defined carefully in relation not only to the physical fears and possible hostility they generate, but to the obstacles they also create for individuals who want to imagine and pursue different purposes.

We might, for example, object to pornography for two interesting reasons: 1. The way pornographic images especially in hard-core or "aggressive" porn "assault my projected image of myself as an individual (woman) worthy of inviolability and able to imagine and reimagine my own bodily integrity," as Cornell thinks and 2. how publicly and pervasively displayed pornography creates "one imaginary" and "makes it appear the truth of 'sex' . . . in other words, the images are those that have been encoded as the truth of our 'sex' in a heterosexual masculine symbolic" (1995, 148). Together these would violate opportunities for important multiple conceptions of oneself and one's goals and life plans. Another passage helps elaborate:

> In the case of violent pornography, the symbolism of the women in bits and pieces, as bodies which are not only violable but there to be violated, assault me immediately. It assaults my projected image of myself as an individual worthy of inviolability and able to imagine and reimagine my own bodily integrity. To strip someone forcibly of her self image, particularly when that image is as basic as that of bodily integrity, is a violation. When a woman is forced to see her "sex" ripped apart, this interferes with her ability to construct an imaginary domain for herself. But I want to emphasize again that it is not just the confrontation with the images in and of themselves. It is the confrontation with the images in their inevitability, because they are allowed to pervade our public space so thoroughly, that itself constitutes the violation. I cannot help but be an enforced viewer of this one pornographic scene. In other words, the images are those that have been encoded as the truth of our 'sex' in heterosexual masculine symbolic. I am arguing that it is the encoding of these images, through their domination of public space, that makes them seem as if they were the truth of sex and not just one particular imaginary (148).

Regulation of such degrading imagery could follow, then, to protect something like self-esteem. But we should conceive of a law that still leaves room for acknowledgment of a multitude of fantasies, a plurality of political reactions to pornography, and the possibility that some may find desirable what many consider pornographic. Why stifle experimentation, especially among individuals whose self projections remain marginalized by the dominant culture? A response to pornography that would regulate it via zoning codes could look attractive. And codes could zone such that "certain images cannot be displayed so that they are unavoidable if one happens to be on a particular street or in a particular part of town" (147). The goal would be to ensure that no one has to see pornography who does not want to.

This is not the kind of argument that depends upon claims for "public decency" around certain buildings. Certainly we could identify secondary effects associated with activities around some pornography stores, but a balance has to be struck. The key here lies in recognizing pornography as more than simply "offensive" at times, and to focus on regulations that create space for more diverse (sexual) projections. Again, "the wrong of pornography being 'in my face'" and the ways in which "enforced confrontation with an image, which potentially assaults a woman's psychic projection of herself as inviolable, as worthy of personhood," are what make a difference. "When I have thrust upon me a fantasy of my body," Cornell writes, "that completely undermines my own imaginary projection of bodily integrity, I am at that moment harmed because it undermines my ability to imagine myself as a person worthy of happiness, whose minimum conditions of individuation deserve to be protected equally. I am forced to view myself as a degraded 'sex'" (149-150). Zoning that shows caution but acknowledges an important complaint may determine that an adult video store would have to take care in the way they create street displays (150). But going further would be treacherous because we cannot begin to prescribe how everyone's fundamental sexual projections of themselves might function. We should never consider simply banning access to Hustler or an adult gay book store or any other experimental efforts to play out adult sexual fantasies.

Brison and Cornell provide additional reasons to envision a description of free agency that accounts for choice while acknowledging physical integrity with its complex links to inner perceptions, projections and fears. This limited effort to talk about agency in a more multi-dimensional way does not lead to a list of necessary goods or capability functionings. The presumption that we must take into account links between physical and emotional integrity, language and self-esteem, does not direct peoples' emotional life or imagined futures. The link reminds us less about how to shape life and more about the possible protections needed to make as much space as possible for unfettered agency-centered expression.

However, another problem crops up with this. Does protection of physical integrity and self-esteem present the possibility that every offensive image will be scrutinized, every flag ever flown over a country conducting violent acts be banished from public display? The argument suggests such points may be raised. It suggests that discussions can reasonably take place around certain symbols, keeping in mind that the most important thing here remains protection against significant, ongoing fears of physical harm and degradation. Protections in this arena should be reviewed on a case-by-case basis, not expecting the comments above to provide one overarching procedure for decision making. It seems to me that a distinction, drawn from Thomas Nagel, remains helpful to keep in mind. Nagel talks about both the distinction between an offense that one can escape from and an offense forced on a person (1991, ch. 14, 166-67). Cornell picks up on this point, writing that this distinction allows us to argue further, for example, "that there is a difference between an offense to someone who just can't bear the idea that homosexuals live in society and to a woman who must confront pornography which is "in her face" (1995, 149). Pornography has been used to project qualities that degrade and objectify and it is inescapably on every newsstand and in every video store. However, what exactly happens when a person who opposes homosexuality has to live with the thought that others are in same-sex unions? Not much, many would claim. The person who claims that same-sex unions are offensive or even sinful may find him or herself around gay co-workers but that person need not be forced to repeatedly confront pictures of activity where dismemberment of overtly heterosexual individuals is occurring simply because those individuals are heterosexual and objects to be viewed as such. Most importantly, any offended person in this case is never asked to give up their chance to have their own sexual fantasies. The acknowledgment that a same-sex union exists need not lead to pervasive and explicit degradation of others' choices or intimidation of others' bodies.[2]

Oakeshott on Self-Enactment

Oakeshott would be concerned about the modifications I make to agency. However, he does discuss the importance of something called agency "self-enactment," and describes the latter through reference to a person's inner world, to the motives of action and their importance to describing agency conduct. How does acknowledgment of self-enactment help support the points made thus far?

An answer requires fuller appreciation of self-enactment and its relation to what Oakeshott calls self-disclosure. The latter refers to something humans do whenever pursuing their wants or goals (which in turn take into account the prescriptive principles that, like "prevailing winds," exist as we set about "sailing (our) several courses" through life (1975, 70)). Self-disclosure is about performances "in respect of their being responsive to contingent situations conducive to the achievement of imagined outcomes" (70). Self-enactment, on the other hand is more about the sentiments in which actions are chosen and performed. These are not simply "organic impulses or urges" or psychological states. Oakeshott sees enactment distinctly "emancipated from liability to the frustration of adverse circumstances" (73); it has more to do with an agent's own sense of integrity or honor. The "compunctions it enjoins are not concerned with recognizing agency in others but with an agent's exercise of his powers of agency in respect of himself" (75). Hence, enactment is "a language in which conduct may be recognized in terms of its 'virtue' and an agent may recognize himself in respect of his 'virtuousness'" (75).

But what exactly shapes this virtuousness? No single categorical imperative explains it. And it is "not to be confused with 'altruistic' conduct." Rather "this expression and its likes refer to the quite different considerations of actions in respect of their intended consequences, while 'honor,' 'integrity'. . . [enactment] which is the consideration here, is totally indifferent to consequences of any sort" (76). Moreover, "conduct which notably fails to observe this condition is shameful" as opposed to guilty (76-77). Self-enactment may not be about "conscience." It is, however, about a sense of inner integrity. And it has a kind of durability that humans appear to desire.

This reinforces how an agent's perceptions of self matter. But significant resistance to any collective protection of self-enactment would emerge from an Oakeshottian concern about privacy. On the one hand, self-enactment is never totally a private language, so to speak. "We" often have something to say about what makes for virtuous conduct and the conditions for shame. "Our moral language may often be confused in its identification of 'virtuous' or 'vicious' sentiments, but it is not undecided whether or not to applaud malice or to disapprobate a motive of good faith or generosity" (77). And "we are not indifferent to each other's exploits in self-enactment, we readily admire noble self enactment when we discern it, and we have more confidence, for example, in the man whose subscriptions to his obligations seem to be made in good faith rather than in fear" (77). But, Oakeshott continues with the following:

> our concern with the sentiment in which the action of another is performed is limited by recognition of our hardly avoidable ignorance and by the conviction that in ordinary human intercourse a man's choices of what to do and the compunctions they exhibit matter more than the sentiment in which he makes them. In respect of motives, it is appropriate that we should take our fellows as we find them; not 'judging' them (as we sometimes have to judge their self-disclosures), but contemplating them with admiration, with reserve, or with indulgence (77).

Caution toward the inner life is in order. (Oakeshott even suggests that through self-enactment "doing is delivered, at least in part, from the deadliness of doing, a deliverance gracefully enjoyed in the quiet of a religious faith" (74).)

We can support these points, however, and still acknowledge the way practices affect a range of considerations including self-esteem. As stated earlier, we care about whether an action is performed in good faith or with fear. Acknowledging how fear forms, and may be prevented where possible, does not mean that we must insist on judging all conduct based on motives that we often cannot discern. It means that ways in which one tries to self-enact hold importance. We can consider assessing harms to opportunities for conduct based on a range of obstacles that prevent the development of such a dimension of worthy conduct. No doubt imagined or wished-for satisfactions have little chance to emerge or feel like they matter if one's inner integrity diminishes too dramatically. Moreover, if self-enactment is a "language", then it is never perfectly "private." As Oakeshott admits:

> the fashionable so-called 'morality of conscience' in which good conduct is identified with the contingent self-approval of the agent concerned is no less preposterous in relation to self-enactment in motive than it is in respect of self-disclosure in action. For, although a man's integrity is certainly something which, if he loses it, he loses all, and although this part of moral agency must include a graceful submission (or, on rare occasions, a fierce adherence) to the qualities which belong to his own character if this is required to keep himself intact, this knowing how to be loyal to himself is not a specification of worthy

self enactment but a postulate of moral conduct. The sentiments in which he acts must be emblems of his self-command if they are to contribute to his self-enactment, but the quality of that self-enactment will depend upon the quality of these sentiments in terms of their subscriptions to a moral practice. . . . There is nothing 'merely subjective' in motives" (75).

We are reminded that self-enactment is never merely subjective. But as valuable, or so much the emancipated core of the self, and the locus of poetic, non-instrumental activity, it makes little sense to ignore how the rules and practices we share affect it.

But let's say that my concerns are convincing. Again, how can agency be more responsive to self-esteem or self-enactment protections and still stand reasonably open to moral pluralism? Clearly the answer takes us back to the policy examples cited. The notion of agency I describe remains more responsive to talking about conditions for freedom, but wary of listing a set of needs or goods or common functionings. And the conditions focus on targets for harms, but then suggest that identifying exact harms to prevent diminished capacities for agency will depend upon the examples or spheres of activity in which we operate.

Besides this, several interconnected considerations need attention. Moral pluralism appeared less likely to flourish when we were presupposing that free citizens must exercise an ethic of equality based on mutual respect leading to reciprocity. Civil regard, an alternative ethic, seemed more conducive to sustaining different moral perspectives. But the latter was limited and identified with problems in Oakeshott. Given my concerns, can another option find expression?

Toward Responsive Regard

Enlarged Appreciation and Disregard

I want to augment the strengths of civil regard (as discussed in chapter 5), but ask civil regard to provide opportunities for a more responsive reaction to collective repairing and renewing of shared practices that, when left alone or expected to change gradually, often become dangerous and harmful in relation to the problems discussed above. Civil regard might acknowledge my "domestic partner," for example, by encouraging acknowledgment of him as an equal agent, asking that others resist the temptation to convert him to believing in state or religiously condoned marriage vows. But responsive regard would ask for more. It might encourage acknowledgment that certain public policies, left as they are, create undue obstacles impeding my partner's reasonably conceived purposes. We may need to show concern for how he and others are currently prevented access to using certain common rules—how they may not receive visitation rights when a partner or relative is ill; how they may face difficulties inheriting property or sharing health benefits. Adding responsivity to regard explores a fuller ethic.

Two specific tactics augment civil regard, making it more responsive to agency. First, I would add that the underlying assumptions supporting civil regard should include the fact that we intelligently use language and properly learn civil adverbial rules alongside the ability to not only use language poetically and politely but with irreverence and provocation. Moreover, we can explore the latter without compromising too dramatically the fragile web of interconnectivity that prevents violence (even if the connections do not always promote full cooperation and certainly prompt civil disobedience or other tactics for challenging authority). In the midst of strong moral pluralism, we may not only bridge gaps between us using civil politeness, but may find ourselves capable of enlarged appreciation for one another as we witness various tactics for questioning existing rules and norms. We never stand aside fully from the language we learn nor can we resist its requests completely. We need to know the rules of a practice in order to question and confound or reform. But displays of disregard protesting adverbial considerations must be possible. Practices are never just neutral games like chess or baseball (as Oakeshott often wants to claim). They have a political past of which we must remain vigilantly aware.

Responsive regard, then, starts with additional expectations when compared to civil regard—it broadens expectations about how humans can challenge as well as trust the language they use. It suggests the need to appreciate how all of us may be capable of testifying to our experiences and communicating these to others who can be responsive listeners. Understanding may not occur easily if moral differences are strong. But if we see ourselves as agents in the way described above, I believe we should maintain active listening and attention to the harms against physical integrity and self-esteem that formal guidelines (or a lack of them) within a practice may enhance or ignore. Appreciating such testimony does not require seeing the world fully from another's point of view; nor deeply understanding how they feel. Responsive regard should provide an option for reaching out, but in a way that neither lets practices be nor sees language as a revelatory medium for exchange.

Responsive regard can look feasible and desirable in any number of situations. Take a situation where a group of women want to protest policies about street safety. They may want more active public protection or hope to protest a community's lack of response to assault complaints. The group may want men engaged in the protest, though some may claim that no man will ever fully "understand" where they are coming from, how it feels to live in a body constructed as "feminine." On this view, heterosexual men in particular should be excluded from a political coalition. At best, they can sit by politely or inquisitively and not interfere with protests. The approach is understandable, but another alternative could involve concerned others sharing some experiences with them while not expecting to elicit full understanding. In offering testimony one could try to demonstrate why the practices we live with (and tacitly acquiesce to) are the responsibility of all community members and need alteration in order to avoid harms preventing some from having an equal chance to exercise agency and imagine a future. One can look to elicit a responsive mode of regard for others' agency harms and use this for bridging differences and prompting collective action on a specific issue.

In more difficult situations, responsive regard can look less plausible than civil regard. Debates about preventing discrimination in the workplace based on sexual orientation are often misconstrued as dealing with "special rights," and have led to so much acrimony that a dose of civility between various groups is sometimes the best one can hope for. However, while valuable to insist that in such charged discussions people avoid yelling or dismissing other's remarks out of hand, it looks rather ineffectual and troublesome to leave things at this level if significant harms occur as people lose their jobs over irrelevant criteria. Responsive regard, committed to recognition of our equal capacities (and implicitly to an equal chance to pursue those capacities) for agency, will ask us to remain open to a collective problem here. It would ask for openness toward testimony about the disregard shown in the workplace, about the harms that certain demands generate. And it would ask for formal review of the implications that all will face if we agree to empower managers in a workplace to scrutinize certain sexual activities that have no bearing on work performance. Adverbial considerations must remain open to augmentation and reevaluation even if we do not fully understand or support the life plans' and desires of others engaged in the same practice. Responsive listening to testimony hopes that we may still enlarge appreciation for what others want to avoid (at the very least). This may stimulate more support for their causes, bring their testimony to other settings, show concern about shared practices even as we feel unable to speak in the other's name. There is nothing shameful about this cautious recognition. It presents possibilities for political action alongside a responsible acknowledgment of limitations.

Crossover Coalitions

Having highlighted two features that distinguish responsive regard from civil regard, I wish to identify a third. As noted, responsive regard requires a certain view of language and a skepticism about rules; it requests a willingness to enlarge appreciation for testimony from others especially about harms experienced in shared practices. A third characteristic relates to these expectations. It has to do with coalition building for political action. Democratic mutual respect was identified with fair cooperation and convergence between different others. Oakeshottian regard promoted what I would call coexistence based on a contingent coming together of various practitioners. Responsive regard could accomplish something more like coalition building. I want to clarify my expectations again by comparing them with a democratic and conservative alternative. I will then highlight thoughts about coalition building from writers well aware of difficulties faced by those pursuing emancipatory political action yet committed to acknowledge abiding differences.

First, what is meant by identifying deliberative democracy with convergence? Deliberative democrats would reject this label. In *Democracy and Disagreement*, Gutmann and Thompson offer a chart (1996, 53) that characterizes the goal of reciprocity as "deliberation agreement/disagreement." This label is meant to create distance from convergence and receptivity to diversity and dissent. It is supposed to express appreciation for a tension summed up in the following passage: "The more general features of society discussed earlier—scarcity of resources, limited generosity, incompatible values and incomplete understanding—sometimes preclude deliberative agreement. But even in the face of what we call deliberative disagreement, reciprocity calls on citizens to continue to seek fair terms of social cooperation among equals" (53). Deliberative democrats try to balance competition and cooperation here; their goal resists eliminating the former for the latter.

However, I would stand by characterizing the deliberative democratic position as more inclined toward convergence and less likely to appreciate strong moral pluralism. As discussed in chapter 3, I believe democratic reciprocity marked by mutual respect aims toward lasting cooperative arrangements guided by transformative civic magnanimity. When we see this put into practice through deliberative democratic examples, conditions that challenge cooperation are overcome, common ground emerges, and mutually justifiable, morally significant foundations for public policy arrangements are established. More importantly, however, deliberative democrats present reciprocity as providing cooperative results that differ only from two rivals. On the one extreme stand those supporting a principle of prudence leading to bargaining that produces a modus vivendi. On the other extreme we find those subscribing to the principle of impartiality and attempting to universally demonstrate one morally correct point of view for grounding public policy and law. With these poles presented, reciprocity looks more attractive and balanced. A modus vivendi remains highly skeptical of resolving moral disagreements on mutually justifiable grounds. An impartial cooperative arrangement assures us that reason can overcome a wide range of human differences, not through bargaining or deliberation but through what Gutmann and Thompson call demonstration "which aims insofar as possible to establish the truth of a comprehensive moral view" (1996, 54). But if other options recognize the depth of moral disagreement and provide different cooperative arrangements between a modus vivendi and comprehensive consensus, deliberative democracy cannot claim exclusive standing. In relation to a range of possibilities now on the table, deliberative reciprocity presents a reasonable option but more likely generates convergence and comparatively fewer contingent cooperative arrangements.

What about contingent coexistence? How does this compare? In *On Human Conduct*, Oakeshott's first chapter on agency and understanding concludes with a discussion of the ideal relationship between moral practices bound through civility. He describes this ideal relationship as marked by contingency. The latter produces the following interconnections between us:

The most exiguous form of such a relationship may be called "incidental." Here, a falling together of such occurrences is understood to intimate a dependent relationship and recognition of it thus to enhance the intelligibility of the occurrences, not because there is any assigned reason why they should have fallen together, nor because there is any noticeable "fit", but merely because having fallen together they do not repulse one another. They are recognized to hold together rather than identified as belonging together. . . .

A contingent relationship in the full sense, however, is a sequential relationship of intelligent individual occurrences where what comes after is recognized to be conditional upon what went before, not merely because before and after cannot here be reversed, nor (of course) because what went before is recognized as a casual condition or because they are recognized to be functionally related, but because they "touch" and in touching identify themselves as belonging together and as composing an intelligible continuity of conditionally dependent occurrence. (1975, 104).

For Oakeshott, civil regard does not instigate a bargain. It leads to formal relationships that invite active responses and appreciation of individuals' intelligence. It is "contextual": "to understand a substantive performance in which an agent discloses and enacts himself is to put it into a story in which it is recognized to be an occurrence contingently related to other occurrences" (105). This can lead to incidental or rather tenuous relationships, to much more tightly woven, deeply interrelated occurrences that form a series of responses and complementary related maneuvers. What this lacks, however, is talk of any rational procedure linking practices or persons and leading to an "unconditional conclusion" (105). It speaks of "holding together" through civility leading to a range of invitations to continue speaking and interacting. It can never stand secure on common goals, moral consensus, or mutually justifiable moral understandings. In comparison with deliberative democracy, this does look like a more partial goal, perhaps better able to allow diverse displays even as individuals or groups coexist.

But what about coalition building? What can it offer that Oakeshott's view lacks? I claimed that my description of agency, integrity, and protests to practices should multiply opportunities to acknowledge the intelligence of others and generate concern for more complex kinds of harms; so coalition building, even in the face of strong moral pluralism, should request more than contingent "touching." It will ask us to take more action together and more responsibility for pressing change in the practices we share. Coalitions envision a coalescing of individuals into action and into a range of more broadly based political acts than Oakeshott has in mind. Coalition building should have affinities with what Nancie Caraway describes as "crossover politics."

Caraway, in the final chapter of her *Segregated Sisterhood* (1991), imagines a multicultural feminist politics, supportive of democracy and strategies for emancipatory change. She avoids detailed reconstruction of personhood or an equality ethic like responsive regard. But she urges "principled affinities" between diverse women and imagines ways of listening, encountering the stories of distinct lives, and of possibly "crossing over" toward others while searching for tentative reasons to change rules and challenge public arrangements. Caraway uses a "crossover" metaphor while remaining attentive to the dangers of assimilation. Here's how she explores the metaphor:

> Crossover politics implies that all parties shift a bit—not forever, but strategically for survival and health. Crossover feminists try (but never truly succeed) to see and hear from "other" vantage points, perhaps sharing some of their experience and knowledge with someone else some of whose own experience and knowledge might rub off. Hopes for such empathetic transfers are restrained, however—viewed as welcomed long shots. Because it understands the fragility and limits of reciprocity and mutuality ("put yourself in my shoes"), a feminist crossover community does not draw on the affective models of "organic" collectivities. The histories of segregated "sisterhood" have made as all too wary of these metaphors. Although appealing, such visions of bonding often mask impulses toward conformity, toward silencing differences, dissent, and even "deviance." A crossover model of community is more socially modest, encouraging unassimilated others in somewhat distant but ultimately more egalitarian structures. "Crossovering" requires not a shedding of one's own particular roots but a willingness to acknowledge the cultural life world contained in someone else's roots. It is neither a hierarchical nor an assimilative metaphor—taboos to keep us constantly alert—nor does it aim for a dialectical, higher social whole or an unwrinkled unity. The music which gets created in crossover tones is usually hyphenated in genre, far from pure, like "our" lives. The crossover styles are open to an encouraging mixing, playing around, experimenting. Processed-driven, crossover "we"s know that we will never get it "just right"; we reject the priests and saviors who preach correctness (171-72).

The crossover image emphasizes reaching out by sharing and listening and shifting "a bit" based on the stories one encounters. But it expects modest steps as one shows consideration and interest for others. It does not expect too much too quickly. We cannot always get the other "right." We might do better to hope that through encounters "in the flesh" something will "rub off." It also suggests how concern for others may be desirable after we get to know their stories. But empathy cannot be a requirement; it may be a "long shot" when forming collective arrangements. Efforts to crossover are often associated with more egalitarian structures, but this is also not taken in the spirit of pining for "sisterhood," nor should we expect "organic collectivities" or even immediate overlapping consensus. Reciprocity and mutuality are fragile hopes when differences are strong. Tentative collaborations are possible; mixing and experimental "playing around" can produce cross pollination and coalition building.[3]

Caraway leaves room for us to display ourselves, to offer ideas, and to keep conversation going. There is interest in coexistence but not a sense that we must forsake change and political action in order to accommodate diversity.

Alongside these points, I can offer another clarification. I said previously that coalitions emerging from responsive regard could be "concerned about" others and the world we share. This does not mean that individuals acting with civil regard and promoting coexistence or individuals acting with reciprocity and hoping to converge with different others show little or no concern for their world. But listening coupled with concern as the underlying motivation for coalition building can look distinctive. It stands out in contrast to the complacency or comfort marking contingent "touching" or attempts to systematize the rules that we have; it does not expect us to feel like or feel for others based on transformed understandings or our ability to transcend particular perspectives. It suggests a level of interest, even a watchful anxiety related to the conditions our society constructs and how these affect access to the practices we all may use in the future. To demonstrate such concern does not mean that we immediately know enough to "take care of" others, although this has some affinities with the ethic of care Joan Tronto discusses as "a species activity that includes everything that we do to maintain, continue, and repair our world so that we can live in it as well as possible" (1993, 103). Its approach must acknowledge how new variations between groups will emerge and politics will require such rearrangements as situations change.

Having offered coalition building as the potential goal of responsive regard, we still need to ask: If coalitions do not aim for anything close to complete consensus, how will they justify any public goods or stable public policies? How will responsive regard lend itself to what looks like a proper appreciation for the ambiguity of authority (something that chapter 3 especially suggested remains critical to sustaining moral pluralism) yet propose authoritative rules that any thinker (other than an anarchist perhaps) would want?

Pluralism, Authority, and the Authoritative

To approach this issue about authority and its accommodations of moral pluralism, I would begin by clarifying one further distinction: the difference between law and politics. The distinction helps sharpen my answer to the questions above as well as establish a final set of contrasts between my ideas and those of others.

Law is often defined by a number of features. We recognize it as a "rule or order that it is advisable or obligatory to observe" and enforced by some kind of controlling authority. Or again "law implies imposition by a sovereign authority and the obligation of obedience on the part of all subject to that authority." We often further distinguish it in contrast to other requests and demands that flow from rules, regulations, statutes, precepts, etc. A rule "applies to more restricted or specific situations," like the rules of a game. A regulation may imply "prescription by authority in order to control an organization or system," like regulations affecting state environmental protection agencies. A precept "commonly suggests something advisory and not obligatory communicated typically by teaching" (Webster's New Collegiate Dictionary, 10th, ed., 659). And so forth.

Politics, on the other hand, is generally activity marked by contestation and debate between our varied and variable reasons for the rules, laws, regulations and in some cases, the social norms that we plan to adopt or reject, applaud or dismiss. It refers to the dynamic, sometimes more systematic and governmentally shaped efforts we make to think and speak about the authoritative prescriptions shaping our lives.

In many cases, the way we construct the contours of "the political" is what provides enough space for moral pluralism to flourish. This does not mean that pluralism receives no breathing room when politics is of limited interest, when we are given significant space (marked by limited interference) to engage in religious worship, to establish guidelines for our children at home, to banter in the "marketplace" with friends. However, in addition to these domains, we often prize the opportunities accorded to us to present and discuss publicly our contending options for re-thinking or altering common norms. Making this space vibrant ultimately remains a crucial way to take moral pluralism as seriously as possible; it makes sure that new ideas for change are not submerged but rather have the opportunity to join others to keep authority on guard, so to speak, and add to rules currently considered authoritative.

Both deliberative democrats and more conservative thinkers like Oakeshott are concerned about the political. For Oakeshott politics could be lively, but it must be highly circumscribed. Politics is "an engagement concerned with the desirability or otherwise of the authoritative prescriptions of respublica and with nothing else" (1975, 170). Because any civil association is itself formulated in terms of rules "indifferent to the merits of any interest or to the truth or error of any beliefs and consequently not itself a substantive interest or doctrine" (170), political deliberation about such rules must remain civil and concerned solely with formal arrangements. Perhaps the saving grace of this view is that authority so conceived cannot promote the civil obligation "to acknowledge the truth or the falsity of a theorem or a doctrine. There is not even the obligation to believe the prescriptions of lex (or law) to be desirable or to approve of them" (171). But while this may be so, and "there is nothing in the engagement (of politics) itself which calls for or excludes particular places or occasion" (166), there is never an instrumental component to political discussion. Anything believed to be morally right or wrong or "organically beneficial or harmful to human beings" (170), anything that seems even like "an affront to civil freedom" (170) is denied status as a rightly conceived political concern. And of course, for Oakeshott, all of this is coupled with the demand that one must acquiesce to authority even as one remains critical. To dissent from authority "is not merely to refuse to subscribe to conditions specified in lex, it is to deny civil obligation and to extinguish civil intercourse and with it the possibility of reflecting upon its conditions in terms of their desirability . . . [it] is giving notice of a resolve to terminate civil association, and genuine dissentients are either secessionist . . . or they are disposed to destroy the civil condition in civil war" (164). (Hobbes looms large here.) Acquiescence to authority is necessary but its legitimacy is based on its neutrality.

This limited, neutral expectation for political discussion as well as for the obligations set by law should keep diversity alive. That is the Oakeshottian option. Deliberative democrats clearly see the situation differently. They consider it implausible to strive for such strict, ideal formality. So while impartial moral conclusions cannot be rationally deduced and used as the basis for public rules, certain morally justifiable common understandings can be developed wisely and fairly and used to support the legitimization of civil conditions. Politics must become a focused endeavor for working out details of moral accommodation, for recognizing our differences but ultimately synthesizing our perspectives such that we can trust one constructed perspective as properly representative of us. Once this is done, law may not be neutral, but we can obey its commands with greater comfort. Politics is conducted for the sake of substantively grounding the law. If we are going to obey such rules at all, they might as well be morally defensible.

From my perspective, we are unlikely to sustain strict neutrality but this is because I would immediately recognize that an "ontological intervention" (Cornell 1995) takes place as soon as I or anyone else establishes expectations about equality in relation to a view of agency and freedom. Neither Oakeshott's view nor mine nor anyone else's view of agency is perfectly neutral. Indeed, my own conception is clearly concerned about freedom, clearly concerned about self-esteem, clearly based on certain psychological observations and open to review. Law that fails to acknowledge these considerations fails to acknowledge that it has some valued purposes. So, I can imagine supporting a certain substantive yet limited backing for general rules directed toward agency protection of integrity and self-esteem.

Does this mean that my idea of politics is just one step away from simply rearranging our expectations about the way civil guidelines allow for the expression of agency as conceived? The answer is both yes and no. Clearly politics could be concerned about discussing, debating, and distributing the protections we associate with being able to have an equal chance to pursue agency. But now I would say (moving yet further away from the formal view) that politics can and should be about more. And this is because the realm of what we contest as authoritative consists of more then simply "laws" strictly understood. Politics may be about the desirability of a great range of rules, regulations, precepts which make varied obligatory demands. It may be about rules governing economic demands, goods, and services as well. To be concerned about these, means that we should imagine politics leading to debate about a much broader set of concerns related to "the authoritative" (Flathman 1980). It also means that a plurality of positions should have greater room for expression and experimentation.

This latter point brings us back to deliberative democracy. Even as I reject a perfectly neutral set of expectations for promoting pluralism in politics and law neither do I want to invest law with the kind of moral foundation deliberative democrats pursue. That does not mean I never trust efforts to converge on tentative moral justifications for new public policies. But we might have to live with fewer rules or at least with the status of law receiving less of the justificatory power deliberative democrats discuss. Nonetheless, room can exist for conver gence as we debate certain regulations, think about how to organize into unions, consider challenging the curriculum in a neighborhood school, test how far our commonalities take us. During significant disagreement, again I can imagine civility guidelines in play. The key is to recognize the ways in which different efforts to legitimate may prove situation specific, supporting rules and obligations of varying weight. If the rules that concern us have the status of law, we may, indeed, be more concerned to legitimate obligations through our agreements about certain harms but then remain responsive to forming coalitions open to further tentative agreements. But again, because politics itself is not so limited and because its target should involve questions about more than legal arrangements, many options for it should emerge.

I clearly believe that my efforts to provide another characterization of agency and an attitude toward others are worth placing on the register of possibilities. I am especially supportive of the option because of its preoccupation with reconciling a common conception of our capacities for freedom alongside fairness.

There is a liberal cast to my ideas. But my position is coupled with certain expectations often downplayed by liberals as well as a broadening of the realm of the political so as to maintain the kind of questioning, contestation and collective action that democracy values. Some, however, might see more liberal expectations here than acknowledged—especially with links to Rawls. More specifically, haven't I attempted to support agency by making its common characteristics limited in scope, less than metaphysical and based on a western model of freedom "for us"? If I have not done this directly, hasn't it been implied?

I would claim that my view of agency not only differs from Rawls's in content but that it has different expectations for its application. My conception of agency should support limiting principles, but it is not necessarily limited in scope. I have not claimed that my concerns about agency will only lead to a list of rights simply identifiable as constitutional essentials. Moreover, I have not tried to pretend that my conception of freedom is neutral. It is one of many possible renderings of freedom, although I would claim that, depending upon one's expectations for moral pluralism, certain conceptions of freedom will look much more appealing than others.

Finally while the weight I have placed upon agency will not find allies in every society, valuing physical integrity and resisting forms of degradation need not be confined to "western societies" alone. My formulations remain somewhat dependent upon a cultural context. Perhaps we can acknowledge their biases while imagining them available for extension and reconfiguration by others. Certainly the case has been made for demonstrating caution in identifying universal assumptions about freedom and the things everyone may call harms. Indeed, one group in a society may see degradation prevention bound up with demands that no bodies, male or female, face sexual servitude; others might start by preventing physical threats surrounding efforts to vote. Whatever the interpretation, these concerns require formulation based on the ordinary transactions within a particular society. But even so, I do think that a less demanding under-standing of freedom focused on protecting against loss of physical integrity and degradation can encourage cross-cultural questions—or encourage individuals in other societies to use such ideas to identify the harms and disturbing conditions they believe thwart their own life choices and chances.[4] I see no reason why others could not make pleas on their own behalf by applying these ideas in their own ways to protect civil liberties. We can, simultaneously, consider crossover coalitions and a responsive stance toward those who make such claims. These are not unfamiliar points—and as I see it, when formulated with a certain sensi-tivity, they may not have to be bound up with condescension or attempts to con-vert others to our "way of life."[5]

Another final note. Some would charge that (like Rawlsian liberals) I have now become engrossed in concerns about cultural justice at the expense of dis-tributive justice.[6] As Nancy Fraser might say, it looks like the emphasis here follows many liberals and communitarian of late who "decouple" their interest in accommodating moral diversity from achieving economic arrangements criti-cal to also reaching fairness (1997, ch. 1). (After all, economic injustice is often the basis of disrespect, resentments, or hostility toward others.) To answer, I would reemphasize how my discussion of the equal standing of purposive agents, who share the capacity for situated, practice-bound choice, implies the need for equivalent access to rules and to the resources necessary to participate in a particular practice. This must remain a high-order priority as well. Other-wise individuals cannot promote their purposes effectively, or fairly. No broad, equal opportunity principle, like Rawls's different principle, may flow from valuing agency freedom. But based on valuing situated agency, I would make the case for supporting the identification of access to specific opportunity sets—goods, resources, participatory structures—critical to performance within a practice. Such sets would remain more or less contestable depending upon who participates in a practice and how participants interpret existing needs. But iden-tifying some practice-related set of resources would remain a priority and guidelines ensuring access to these could be linked to the assumptions and ethic discussed here in order to ensure distributive fairness.

Sen and Nussbaum would see this approach falter if it sidestepped estab-lishing a broad threshold of well-being. Opportunity sets would be all too local and traditional. I could say it is true that I am pressing on the hope that situated agents will draw from traditions they participate in to debate which goods em-power effective use of rules and to demand access to those goods for them-selves. To my mind, this approach may foster enough of a general standard to undermine obstacles to well-being and improve standards of living broadly. Many dispossessed individuals (and especially women worldwide, the focus of Nussbaum's worries in her most recent writing, 1999) could reduce oppression considerably by demanding something akin to recognition of agency but doing so within their cultural contexts, and expanding more choice within the specific practices they want to join or alter. Requests for access to resources or modes of participation of numerous institutions will certainly change the chance to flourish. No doubt, many will imagine reforms continuous with their existing ways of life, but this kind of choice may bring critical import to current norms without asking that all become western liberals or divorced from cherished communities.[7]

Overall, this last chapter has aimed to expand on a view of agency, insisting that agency is itself a practice. I suggest that if we value agency, we should take into account the internal and external components of its development. How these will be identified specifically can be left somewhat open. What should be clear is that without attention to the way rules and practices affect a range of conditions, we miss preventing harms and degradations worth limiting. I also reinforced how a more modest notion of agency does not simply lead to formal or stingy attitudes toward others; it can support an ethic of responsive regard toward actors that may prove more generous than Oakeshottian civil regard while less demanding than democratic reciprocity. In this way, agency may fulfill the promise that leads many to support positive freedom positions, even as it remains more cautious than the latter. Finally, I suggest that a shared conception of agency with responsiveness may not promote a fully stable consensus on public principles. But it could generate the flexible, contingent coalitions that help establish authoritative rules while valuing the reexamination of rules and the material that individuals need in order to help keep diversity in public life alive and well.

Notes

1. In part this has to do with my hesitation about Cornell's reliance on Lacan in formulating her understanding of the psyche and sexual identity. Fraser has a particularly compelling discussion on the limits of "Lacanianism" for a feminist agenda (1997, ch. 6).

2. The other obvious problem with trying to translate the offensiveness of certain sexual acts into some kind of legal restriction is that such arguments are often supported by another idea of equality, but one that obviously cannot be used in public life: the idea that we are all gods creatures, created in his or her image, and that the image of God best understood is from one particular text used in one particular tradition. Beside the fact that this argument rejects efforts to discuss the primacy of agency marked by acknowledgment of others as purposive creatures who may or may not be religious, even if we did find this compelling, our society has over time recognized the need to put arguments like this aside, not to say that they are unworthy, but to acknowledge that they are not always effective as the sole basis for sustaining a common set of understandings for a religiously, ethnically, and in many other ways culturally diverse society.

3. A similar approach is endorsed by Maria Lugones and Joshua Price in their 1995 collaborative essay "Dominant Culture: el deseo por un alma pobre (The Desire for an Impoverished Soul)" from *Multiculturalism from the Margins*. These writers provide certain complements to Caraway's gestures. They use their very different experiences in

the United States as starting points for acknowledging just how distinctly they are positioned and able to view their worlds; but they then work together to imagine "the cognitive groundwork" that they and others could use for "living together" in a society disposed "to decision-making that arises from communication across cultures rather than from cultural erasure" (123). In the midst of using two languages at times in their essay and drawing on their different experiences, they nevertheless propose the following "as groundwork for a multicultural society": "living with uncertainty, living with and within complexity, and living with a deep appreciation for conflicting perspectives as a prerequisite for open-ended understanding" (123). Uncertainty for them "requires humility, curiosity, urgency in communication, and a sense of open-endedness to understanding and being understood. It requires a lack of spontaneity in communication as one questions one's own judgment about what one is seeing, thus deferring on-the-spot decisions. It takes time to unravel why people are saying what they are saying or acting the way they are. Even then, one never feels on unshakable ground" (124). Uncertainty in many ways opens up appreciation for complexities. "To attend to multiple perspectives (also with uncertainty) is to be aware of the shadowy, the seemingly insignificant, or the apparently irrelevant ways in which people act. It is to wonder at the silence, at the anger, at the humor, without dismissing it" (124). And open-ended understanding tries to build on the first two points. "As one approaches situations in this way, one does not assume the discussions will end on a common ground, agreement or consensus. One does not assume what is finest about being human is common to us all. Rather, one takes up situations in all of the multiple, rich, subtle, and difficult to articulate actions, perspectives, politics, ironies, kinds of anger, and senses of right and wrong. One gives oneself a lot of time to understand what is transpiring in its complexity" (125). There is an urgent request here not to seek simplistic agreements that "reduce complex and layered possibilities" (125).

4. The charge that this hope still rests on a flawed universal humanist ideal may emerge. But I would return to the point made in the introduction. Many making this charge have demanded attention to agency themselves, and often without explaining how they would reimagine such a claim and strategize clearly about its protection. (As noted, I think Iris Marion Young faces this dilemma.) Another important critic of "ethnocentric universality" and the "inadequate self consciousness about the effect of western scholarship" on assessments about other parts of the world has been Chandra Mohanty. Mohanty, like so many, has opposed the way western thinkers, including feminists, have used dangerous categories to try to make cross-cultural comparisons. The categories often reinforce simple binary patterns—western women are constructed as a group in opposition to a monolithic imagined set of "Third World women"; the latter need liberation using the insights of the former. The objections to such representations have been stated forcefully and repeatedly—these binary oppositions end up being paternalistic, fail to account for the diversity of those in the "Third World", and ultimately fail to account for the expression of agency that takes place even amidst practices that from the "outside" look traditional and "oppressive". Mohanty makes her point in response to western feminists in the following way: "While radical and liberal feminist assumptions of women as a sex class might elucidate today (however inadequately) the autonomy of particular women's struggles in the West, the application of the notion of women as a homogenous category in the third world colonizes and appropriates the pluralities of the simultaneous location of different groups of women in social class and ethnic frameworks; in doing so it ultimately robs them of their historical and political agency. Similarly, many Zed Press authors who ground themselves in the basic analytic strategies of traditional Marxism also implicitly create a 'unity' of women by substituting 'women's activity' for 'labor' as the primary theoretical determinant of women's situation. Here again, women are consti

tuted as a coherent group not on the basis of "natural" qualities or needs but on the basis of the sociological "unity" of their role in domestic production and wage labor" (see Mansbridge and Okin 1994, 99-100/71-72). These critical observations have been important and influential. But Mohanty mentions "agency" above. What does she mean by this? Could she imagine any support for the conception of freedom that I have developed?

5. Cornell seems especially sensitive to this issue in her 1997 collection of essays where she discusses whether the demand for treatment as an equal must read as a "western" demand. She believes "third world feminists" have already answered concerns about this issue and that examples of resistance by women elsewhere, even when expressed collectively and in relation to traditional cultural concepts, can be interpreted as demanding equivalent evaluation of women's contributions and a recognition of women as having plans and purposes emanating from a sense of individual self worth.

6. Rawls's disinterest in the second principle of justice in *Political Liberalism* does seem emblematic of the problem Fraser identifies.

7. See especially the essays in Bauer and Bell (1999). I am also working to develop this argument further in an essay contrasting my support for "women's" international rights with Susan Okin's justification for the same.

Bibliography

Ackerman, Bruce. 1980. *Social Justice in the Liberal State*. New Haven, Conn.: Yale University Press.

————.1989. "Why Dialogue?" *The Journal of Philosophy*. 86 (1): 5-22.

————.1994. "Political Liberalisms." *The Journal of Philosophy*. 91(7): 364-86.

Alejandro, Roberto. 1998. *The Limits of Rawlsian Justice*. Baltimore: Johns Hopkins University Press.

Alexander, Larry, and Maimon Schwarzschild. 1987. "Liberalism, Neutrality, and Equality of Welfare vs. Equality of Resources." *Philosophy and Public Affairs*. 16 (1): 85-110.

Arendt, Hannah. 1959. *The Human Condition*. Garden City, N.Y.: Doubleday.

Aristotle. 1976. *Ethics*. New York: Penguin.

————.1981. *The Politics*. New York: Penguin.

Arneson, Richard. 1989. "Equality and Equal Opportunity for Welfare." *Philosophical Studies*. 56: 77-93.

Bauer, Joanne and Daniel Bell, eds. 1999. *The East Asian Challenge for Human Rights*. Cambridge, U.K.: Cambridge University Press.

Bell, Daniel. 1972. "On Meritocracy and Equality." *The Public Interest*, no. 29: 26-69.

Benhabib, Seyla. 1992. *Situating the Self*. New York: Routledge.

————.1994. "Deliberative Rationality and Models of Democratic Legitimacy." *Constellations*. 1: 1.

Berlin, Isaiah. 1969. *Four Essays on Liberty*. Oxford, U.K.: Oxford University Press.

Bernstein, Richard. 1983. *Beyond Objectivism and Relativism*. Philadelphia: University of Pennsylvania Press.

Bloom, Irene, J. Paul Martin, and Wayne L. Proudfoot, eds. 1996. *Religious Diversity and Human Rights*. New York: Columbia University Press.

Bock, Gisela and Susan James. 1992. *Beyond Equality and Difference*. New York: Routledge.

Bohman, James. 1995. "Public Reason and Cultural Pluralism." *Political Theory*. 23 (2): 253-79.

Brisson, Susan.1997. *Feminists Rethink the Self*. Boulder, Colo.: Westview Press.

Caraway, Nancie. 1991. *Segregated Sisterhood*. Knoxville: University of Tennessee Press.

Cohen, G. E. 1989. "On the Currency of Egalitarian Justice." *Ethics*. 99 (4): 906-44.

Connolly, William. 1969. *The Bias of Pluralism*. New York: Atherton Press.

————.1995a. "Suffering, Justice, and the Politics of Becoming." Manuscript, Political Science Department, Johns Hopkins University.

————.1995b. *The Ethos of Pluralization*. Minneapolis: University of Minnesota Press.

Cornell, Drucilla. 1992a. *The Philosophy of the Limit*. New York: Routledge

————.1992b. "Gender, Sex, and Equivalent Rights." In *Feminists Theorize the Political*. Edited by Judith Butler and John Scott, New York: Routledge.

————.1995. *The Imaginary Domain*. New York: Routledge.

————.1997. *At the Heart of Freedom*. Princeton, N.J.: Princeton University Press.

Cott, Nancy. 1987. *The Grounding of Modern Feminism*. New Haven, Conn.:Yale University Press.

Daniels, Norman. 1990. "Equality of What: Welfare, Resources, or Capabilities?" *Philosophy and Phenomenological Research* 1 (Fall Supplement): 273-96.

Dworkin, Ronald. 1993. *Life's Dominion: An Argument about Abortion, Euthanasia, and Individual Freedom*. New York: Knopf.

Exdell, John. 1994. "Feminism, Fundamentalism, and Liberal Legitimacy." *Canadian Journal of Philosophy*. 24 (3): 441-64.

Fish, Stanley. 1999. *The Trouble with Principle*. Cambridge, Mass.: Harvard University Press.

Fishkin, James. 1991. *Deliberative Democracy*. New Haven, Conn.: Yale University Press.

Flathman, Richard. 1973. *Concepts in Social and Political Philosophy*. New York: Macmillan.

————.1980. "Rights, Needs and Liberalism." *Political Theory*. 8 (3): 319-330.

————.1984. "Culture, Morality and Rights." *Analyse and Kritik*. 6 (1):8-27.

————.1987. *The Philosophy and Politics of Freedom*. Chicago: University of Chicago Press.

————.1993. *Thomas Hobbes: Skepticism, Individuality, and Chastened Politics*. Newbury Park, Calif.: Sage.

Flax, Jane. 1995. "Race/Gender and the Ethics of Difference: A Reply to Okin's 'Gender Inequality and Cultural Differences.'" *Political Theory*. 23 (3): 500-510.

Fraser, Nancy. 1989. *Unruly Practices: Power, Discourse, and Gender in Contemporary Social Theory*. Minneapolis: University of Minnesota Press.

————.1997. *Justice Interruptus*. New York: Routledge.

Gilligan, Carol. 1982. *In a Different Voice*. Cambridge, MA: Harvard University Press.

Griffin, James. 1986. *Well-being*. Oxford, U.K.: Clarendon Press.

Gutmann, Amy. 1987. *Democratic Education.* Princeton, N.J.: Princeton University Press.

———.1993a. "Democracy." In *A Companion to Contemporary Political Philosophy.* Edited by Robert Goodin and Philip Pettit. Oxford, U.K.: Blackwell.

———.1993b. "The Disharmony of Democracy." In *Democratic Community.* Edited by John W. Chapman and Ian Shapiro. New York: New York University Press.

Gutmann, Amy, and Dennis Thompson. 1996. *Democracy and Disagreement.* Cambridge, Mass.: Harvard University Press.

Hampshire, Stuart. 1983. *Morality and Conflict.* Oxford, U.K.: Basil Blackwell.

———.1989. *Innocence and Experience.* Cambridge, Mass: Harvard University Press.

Hobbes, Thomas. 1986. *Leviathan.* Edited with an introduction by C. B. MacPherson. New York: Penguin Classics.

Kant, Immanuel. 1964. *Groundwork of the Metaphysic of Morals.* Translated by H. J. Paton. New York: Harper and Row.

———.1985. *Kant's Political Writings.* Edited by Hans Reiss. New York: Cambridge University Press.

Kukathas, Chandran. 1992. "Are There any Cultural Rights?" *Political Theory.* 20 (1): 105-39.

Kymlicka, Will. 1989. *Liberalism, Community and Culture.* Oxford, U.K.: Clarendon Press.

Larmore, Charles. 1987. *Patterns of Moral Complexity.* Cambridge, U.K: Cambridge University Press.

———.1990. Political Liberalism. *Political Theory.* 18 (3): 339-360.

Locke, John. 1983. *A Letter Concerning Toleration.* Indianapolis, Ind.: Hackett.

Lugones, Maria, and Joshua Price. 1995. "Dominant culture: el deseo por un alma pobre (The Desire for an Impoverished Soul)." In *Multiculturalism from the Margins.* Edited by Dean Harris. Westport, Conn.: Bergin and Garvey.

Lukes, Stephen. 1989. "Relativism in Its Place." In *Rationalism and Relativism.* Edited by Martin Hollis and Stephen Lukes. Cambridge, Mass.: M. I. T. Press.

———.1991. *Moral Conflict and Politics.* Oxford, U.K.: Oxford University Press.

MacIntyre, Alasdair. 1981. *After Virtue.* Notre Dame, Ind.: University of Notre Dame Press.

Mansbridge, Jane, and Susan Moller Okin, eds. 1994. *Feminism, Volume II.* Aldershot, U.K.: Edward Elgar.

Moghadam, Valentine M. ed., 1994. *Identity Politics and Women. Cultural Reassertion and Feminism in International Perspective.* Boulder, Colo.: Westview Press.

Nagel, Thomas. 1991. *Equality and Partiality.* New York: Oxford University Press.

Nussbaum, Martha. 1988a. "Non-Relative Virtues: An Aristotelian Approach." *Midwest Studies in Philosophy.* 13: 33-53.

————.1988b. "Nature, Function and Capability: Aristotle on Political Distribution." *Oxford Studies in Ancient Philosophy*. Supplemental vol. 145-84.

————.1990a. "Aristotelian Social Democracy." In *Liberalism and the Good*. Edited by R. Bruce Douglass, Gerald M. Mara, and Henry S. Richardson. New York: Routledge.

————.1990b. "Our Pasts, Ourselves." *The New Republic*. Vol. 202, Iss. 15, April 9, 27-34.

————.1992. "Human Functioning and Social Justice." *Political Theory*. 20 (2): 202-246.

————.1999. *Sex and Social Justice*. New York: Oxford University Press.

Oakeshott, Michael. 1962. *Rationalism in Politics and Other Essays*. Totowa, N.J.: Rowman & Littlefield.

————.1975. *On Human Conduct*. London: Clarendon Press.

————.1983. *On History*. Totowa, N.J.: Barnes & Noble Books.

Okin, Susan Moller. 1989a. "Reason and Feeling in Thinking about Justice." In *Feminism and Political Theory*. Edited by Cass Sunstein, Chicago: University of Chicago Press.

————.1989b. *Justice, Gender and the Family*. New York: Basic Books.

————.1994. "'Political Liberalism,' Justice and Gender." *Ethics,* 105: 23-43.

Pateman, Carol. 1988. *The Sexual Contract*. Stanford, Calif.: Stanford University Press.

Pennock, J. Roland, and John Chapman, eds. 1967. *Equality*. New York: Atherton Press.

Peters, Julie, and Andrea Wolper. 1995. *Women's Rights, Human Rights*. New York: Routledge.

Rawls, John. 1971. *A Theory of Justice*. Cambridge, Mass.: Harvard University Press.

————.1980. "Kantian Constructivism in Moral Theory: The Dewey Lectures 1980." *The Journal of Philosophy*. 77, 9: 515-72.

————.1996. *Political Liberalism*. New York: Columbia University Press.

————.1993. "The Law of Peoples." In *Human Rights*. Edited by Stephen Shute and Susan Hurley. New York: Basic Books.

Raz, Joseph. 1986. *The Morality of Freedom*. Oxford, U.K.: Oxford University Press.

Rorty, Amelie. 1990. "Varieties of Moral Pluralism in a Polyphonic Society." *Review of Metaphysics*. 44 (September): 3-20.

Rosenblum, Nancy. 1987. "Studying Authority: Keeping Pluralism in Mind." In *Authority Revisited* NOMOS XXIX. Edited by J. Roland Pennock and John W. Chapman. New York: New York University Press

Rousseau, Jean-Jacques. 1987. *On The Social Contract with Geneva Manuscript and Political Economy*. Edited by Roger Masters. Translated by Judith Masters. New York: St. Martin's Press.

Scanlon, Thomas. 1991. "The Moral Basis of Interpersonal Comparisons." In *Interpersonal Comparisons of Well-being*. Edited by Jon Elster and John E Roemer. Cambridge, U.K.: Cambridge University Press.

Schwartzenbach, Sibyl. 1991. "Rawls, Hegel, and Communitarianism." *Political Theory.* 19 (4): 539-571.

Sen, Amartya. 1984. *Resources, Values and Development.* Oxford, U.K.: Blackwell.

———.1985. "Well-being, Agency, and Freedom: The Dewey Lectures 1984." *Journal of Philosophy.* 82: 169-221.

———.1988. "Freedom of Choice: Concept and Content." *European Economic Review.* 32. 269-94.

———.1992. *Inequality Reexamined.* New York: Russell Sage Foundation.

———.1999. *Development as Freedom.* New York: Knopf.

Sen, Amartya, and Bernard Williams eds. 1982. *Utilitarianism and Beyond.* Cambridge, U.K.: Cambridge University Press.

Sextus Empiricus. 1985. *Selections from the Major Writings on Skepticism, Man, and God.* Indianapolis, Ind.: Hackett.

Taylor, Charles. 1975. *Hegel.* Cambridge, U.K.: Cambridge University Press.

———. 1985. *Philosophy and the Human Sciences, Philosophical Papers, volume 2.* Cambridge, U.K.: Cambridge University Press.

———.1989. *Sources of the Self.* Cambridge, Mass.: Harvard University Press.

Tronto, Joan. 1993. *Moral Boundaries.* New York: Routledge.

Van Ness, Peter, ed. 1999. *Debating Human Rights: Critical Essays from the United States and Asia.* London: Routledge.

Waldren, Jeremy. 1991. "The Substance of Equality." *Michigan Law Review.* (May) 89:1350-1370.

Walzer, Michael. 1983. *Spheres of Justice.* New York: Basic Books.

Warren, Mark. 1996. "Deliberative Democracy and Authority." *APSR.* 90 (1): 46-60.

Westen, Peter. 1982. "The Empty Idea of Equality." *Harvard Law Review.* 95 (3):537-596.

———.1990. *Speaking of Equality.* Princeton, N.J.: Princeton University Press

Williams, Bernard. 1962. "The Idea of Equality." Reprinted, 1971 in *Justice and Equality.* Edited by Hugo Bedau, Englewood Cliffs, N.J.: Prentice Hall.

———.1972. *Morality: An Introduction to Ethics.* New York: Harper and Row.

———.1973. Ethical Consistency. In *Moral Dilemmas.* Edited by Christopher Gowens. New York: Oxford University Press.

———.1981. *Moral Luck.* Cambridge, U.K.: Cambridge University Press.

———.1985. *Ethics and the Limits of Philosophy.* Cambridge, Mass.: Harvard University Press.

Wittgenstein, Ludwig. 1953. *Philosophical Investigations.* Translated by G. E. M. Anscombe. New York: MacMillan.

Young, Iris Marion. 1990. *Justice and the Politics of Difference.* Princeton, N.J.: Princeton University Press.

Index

143

About the Author

Ellen Freeberg serves as Director of Academic Affairs and teaches for the Department of Political Science at the Graduate Faculty of New School University. She holds a B.A. from Vassar College and an M.A. and Ph.D. from Johns Hopkins University. She lives in New York City and has taught classes at New York University, Hunter College, and Vassar College.